PYTHON PROGRAMMING FOR BEGINNERS

FROM BASICS TO AI INTEGRATIONS. 5-MINUTE ILLUSTRATED TUTORIALS, CODING HACKS, HANDS-ON EXERCISES & CASE STUDIES TO MASTER PYTHON IN 7 DAYS AND GET PAID MORE

NARRY PRINCE

© Copyright 2023 by Narry Prince- All rights reserved.

This document is geared towards providing exact and reliable information in regard to the topic and issue covered. The publication is sold with the idea that the publisher is not required to render accounting, officially permitted, or otherwise, qualified services. If advice is necessary, legal or professional, a practiced individual in the profession should be ordered.

From a Declaration of Principles which was accepted and approved equally by a Committee of the American Bar Association and a Committee of Publishers and Associations. In no way is it legal to reproduce, duplicate, or transmit any part of this document in either electronic means or in printed format. Recording of this publication is strictly prohibited, and any storage of this document is not allowed unless with written permission from the publisher. All rights reserved.

The information provided herein is stated to be truthful and consistent, in that any liability, in terms of inattention or otherwise, by any usage or abuse of any policies, processes, or directions contained within is the solitary and utter responsibility of the recipient reader. Under no circumstances will any legal responsibility or blame be held against the publisher for any reparation, damages, or monetary loss due to the information herein, either directly or indirectly.

Respective authors own all copyrights not held by the publisher. The information herein is offered for informational purposes solely and is universal as such. The presentation of the information is without a contract or any type of guaranteed assurance. The trademarks that are used are without any consent, and the publication of the trademark is without permission or backing by the trademark owner. All trademarks and brands within this book are for clarifying purposes only and are owned by the owners themselves, not affiliated with this document.

Contents

Introduction — 1

1. The Fundamentals of Python Programming — 5
   The Attributes and Methods in Python

2. Getting Ready To Program With Python — 11
   Shell, IDLE, and Scripts Syntax
   Troubleshooting Installation Issues

3. Variables and Operators in Python — 27
   Creating Variables
   Operators in Python

4. Python Data Types — 60
   Labels
   Applying Variables

5. Breaking Down Lists, Tuples, Sets, and Dictionaries — 74
   Lists
   Tuples
   Sets
   Dictionaries

6. Functions, Modules, and Files in Python — 87
   Functions
   Modules
   Files In Python

7. Object-Oriented Programming Made Easy   97
      The Relationship Between Classes and Objects
      Magic Methods

8. Your First Interactive Program Using Multiline Statements   108

9. Python for Data Analysis   112
      Why Use Python For Data Analysis
      Handling Missing Data

10. Python Data Munging   119
      Why Data Munging Is Important

11. Python Data Munging/Wrangling Exercise   127

12. Inheritance in Python to Clean Your Code   130
      How to Implement Inheritance in Code
      The Super Method

13. Integrating AI and Python Program   136
      Python AI Libraries
      Defining Intelligence—The Five Prerequisites
      Agents and Environments in AI

14. Common Debugging Tools for Seamless Programming   160
      Python Debugging Tools
      Simple But Effective Debugging Tools
      Debugging Best Practices

Conclusion   169

Introduction

When Guido van Rossum released Python in 1991, he had a goal, "to create a programming language that was accessible to everyone." He wanted Python to be an easy and intuitive language that was just as powerful (if not more powerful) than its far more complicated programming language competitors.

Van Rossum may have had a vision, but what Python evolved into, would have almost certainly far exceeded his dreams. Today, the programming language has become a versatile, invaluable tool, standing as a testament to the art of code. Functionality and readability meet squarely with innovation, yet the language remains true to its original promise—simplicity.

Sometimes described as "the Swiss Army knife of programming languages," Python has truly transcended the boundaries of traditional software, evolving into a powerhouse that has transformed the face of modern computing for programmers the world over. From web development to scientific research, artificial intelligence (AI), and data analysis, Python's adaptability knows no bounds.

One of Python's distinguishing features is its elegant and concise syntax—surprisingly close to the English language. It's this quality that makes Python an ideal programming language for beginners as it taps into the human brain's ability to learn other human languages. It is also this "new language" phenomenon that makes it easy to understand Python and what users are programming.

For those wondering why they should learn Python at all, Python's popularity in the programming world has grown exponentially; And for good reason. It comes with a huge number of advantages. These include

- its versatility as a multi-purpose language that is used as the foundation for a wide range of applications.

- a thriving community of developers and an extensive collection of libraries and frameworks that provide you with an abundant number of resources.

- clean and uncluttered code that makes the program easy to read and encourages collaboration.

- a wide range of career opportunities. Python programmers are in high demand in today's economic and job climate.

- open source contribution; which means the program is continually evolving and improving over time.

- scalability which is what you're going to be introduced to in this book—you can start small and gradually build your projects into robust, enterprise-level applications.

Throughout the pages of *INSERT BOOK NAME*, you're going to learn how to unlock Python's full potential. From the foundational concepts that form its core to the advanced techniques that will empower you to create groundbreaking solutions, you're on the precipice of unlocking a world of endless possibilities.

Get ready to uncover,

- Python fundamentals.

- object-oriented programming (OOP).

- web development.

- data manipulation and analysis.

- machine learning and artificial intelligence.

- automation and scripting.

- advanced programming topics.

Embracing the Learning Curve

Before you embark upon your Python journey, there's one piece of critical information you need. Python is, at its core, code, and coding is an art. Like any other art, it requires critical thinking, creativity, and experimentation. While we will certainly provide you with the step-by-step guidance, expert advice, and hands-on exercises needed to become proficient in Python, it's absolutely necessary that you veer off the path from time to time.

We encourage you to learn as much from the theory presented to you as you do through your own trial, error, and failures. For you to truly internalize the concepts that come with Python and develop your problem-solving skills, you're going to need to take the lesser-trodden path.

But, we don't want you to stress, because Python is the ideal language for this great coding adventure. It provides you with a gentle learning curve while still providing you with the powerful tools and capabilities of Python which means you get to learn as you develop.

It's our sincere wish that by the end of this book, you'll be fully equipped to build a fully functional web application where you can process user data, retrieve information from a database, and dynamically display your content. Interactive, responsive, and elegant—a testament to your mastery of Python will be your end goal. But, this accomplishment will only be the beginning of your journey to coding brilliance.

From machine learning to data science and beyond, get ready to transform your life, apply your newfound skills, and accelerate your career possibilities with the limitless potential that is—Python.

CHAPTER 1

The Fundamentals of Python Programming

Python is a programming language that is built on a robust foundation while still offering users simplicity and ease of use. For you to become a Python programming aficionado, it's absolutely critical that you understand the inner workings of Python as a language. It's these fundamentals that we'll be covering in Chapter 1, introducing you to the fundamentals and core concepts that will serve as your base for your skills.

Python is an interpreted language. This means that the code is executed line by line by Python's interpreter. This happens in a process and specific order that includes,

- **Writing Code**—The programmer creates the Python code using a text editor or integrated development environment (IDE). These instructions are written in plain text but follow Python's syntax rules.

- **Compiling vs. Interpreting:** Unlike other programming languages like C++ or Java, Python doesn't require a separate compilation step. Instead, your code is saved as a .py file. The Python interpreter reads and executes this directly.

- **Running the Interpreter:** Next, you'll run your Python code by calling the Python interpreter from the command line or by using an IDE that handles the execution for you. The interpreter reads your code, line by line, and performs the specified actions.

- **Immediate Feedback:** Python then offers you immediate feedback. If there's an error in your code, the interpreter will stop and display an error message. This process allows for quick debugging and learning so that you don't have to read through pages and pages of code.

Before We Begin With Python

Before we begin with the nitty gritty that is Python, I have a gift for you. We know that reading can be a challenge for some of our clients and as such, we've put together an audiobook for you. This book will guide you through the chapters of *Python Programming for Beginners*, allowing you to code along as you listen and learn about this dynamic programming language. All you need to do is scan the QR code below to access your free audiobook.

The Attributes and Methods in Python

Attributes are the characteristics or properties that are associated with an object when programming in Python. Objects, on the other hand, are the core of Python.

Everything in Python is an object—you'll need to keep this in mind for when you start programming in later chapters. An easy way to think of attributes is to equate them to variables that are bound to an object. Let's say you have an object representing a car, its attributes could include color, make, model, and year. You can access these attributes to get information about the object.

```
class Car:
    def __init__(self, make, model, year):
        self.make = make
        self.model = model
        self.year = year
my_car = Car("Toyota", "Camry", 2023)
print(my_car.make)  # Accessing the make attribute
```

Methods, on the other hand, are the functions that are associated with an object. These methods define the behavior of the object and allow you to perform operations on it. Let's carry on with the car example.

A method could be start_engine() to start the car's engine. Methods are defined within classes and are called on instances of those classes.

```
class Car:
    def __init__(self, make, model, year):
        self.make = make
        self.model = model
        self.year = year
    def start_engine(self):
        print(f"The {self.year} {self.make} {self.model}'s engine is now running.")
my_car = Car("Toyota", "Camry", 2023)
my_car.start_engine()  # Calling the start_engine method
```

Once you understand what attributes and methods are, you can begin to organize the building blocks of Python's object-oriented programming language.

As you progress in your Python journey, you'll use them extensively to model real-world concepts and create powerful, interactive applications. With these fundamentals in mind, you'll be better equipped to take a deeper dive into the Python language and its capabilities.

What Python Is Used For and What Can It Do?

Simplicity isn't the only thing Python has to offer; It's a remarkably versatile coding tool. Its language is used in a wide variety of applications across a wide array of domains. This makes it a go-to choice for programmers around the globe. Let's take a closer look at what Python is used for.

Mathematics

An often-overlooked contender for Python is mathematics and the programming language has become a firm favorite with mathematicians, scientists, and engineers across numerous fields and applications. Its rich ecosystem of libraries, including NumPy, SciPy, and SymPy. This makes it the language of choice for complex mathematical and scientific computing because it can handle everything from symbolic mathematics to data analysis and visualization.

Software Development

The simplicity and readability that are hallmarks of Python are incredibly valuable assets for software development. From desktop application creation to games, or mobile apps, Python offers a huge variety of tools and libraries to streamline development processes.

System Scripting

When it comes to system scripting, Python is a natural fit. Its ease of use and cross-platform compatibility make it perfect for automating system-level tasks including file management, process control, and so much more.

Web Development—Server-Side

In the domain of web development, Python has a very strong presence—primarily on the server side. Frameworks like Django and Flask empower developers to create dynamic, feature-rich web applications. It is Python's clear syntax and powerful libraries that make it a top go-to for developers building websites and web services.

When it comes to Python's capabilities, the programming language is used across multiple applications including,

- Web applications on a server to create web applications from simple to sophisticated. Making use of frameworks like Django means developers can build feature-rich, scalable web solutions with ease and efficiency.

- Python can be integrated into current software to create workflows and ensure repetitive tasks are automated. The program is brilliant at connecting the various components of software systems, helping to enhance efficiency and productivity.

- From a database connectivity point of view, Python seamlessly connects to a number of different database systems. These include MySQL, PostgreSQL, MongoDB, and so on. Python can read and modify data in databases, making it a vital tool for data-driven applications.

- Python is adept at working with files because it can easily read, write, and manipulate data stored in files of various formats. This is absolutely essential for data extraction and report generation.

- Python is a data processing master and when combined with libraries like Pandas and NumPy it handles big data like a champ. The language is an absolute powerhouse for data analysis and machine learning, ensuring it keeps its eyes on the future of computing and coding.

- The clear syntax and extensive libraries that are Python's language make it really great for rapid prototyping. This means being able to turn your ideas into functional prototypes, encourages you to iterate and experiment and learn and grow before committing to a large or full-scale project.

- Finally, Python is not just a prototyping software. It's more than capable of producing straight-to-production software because of its scalability and robust nature.

Why Python is Preferred

We're almost ready to have you dive into the world of Python, but first, let's look at why Python is useful outside of the obvious employment opportunities.

1. Python is platform-agnostic. This means it's compatible across various operating systems including Windows, macOS, Linux, and even Raspberry Pi.

2. Its syntax is famously clear and it's this simplicity that enables developers to write code that is maintainable and understandable.

3. The elegant syntax that is synonymous with Python allows developers to achieve far more with far less code actually being written.

4. Python's interpreter system executes code the moment it's written. This means the language promotes rapid prototyping so that you can test and refine your ideas quickly.

5. Python embraces multiple programming paradigms and this means it doesn't matter what you prefer when it comes to coding. From procedural to object-oriented and functional programming, Python prides itself on accommodating your coding style.

Now that you have the *what* and *why* of Python, we can get into the how so that you can begin to code with ease and creativity.

CHAPTER 2

Getting Ready To Program With Python

Part of the solid foundation you need to begin programming with Python includes what version of Python to use as well as how to install the interpreter, and a couple of other crucial factors. This will help you to become comfortable in your Python environment while you explore Python Shell and IDLE.

Python 2.x Verses Python 3.x

So, before you install Python you may be thinking, "What's the difference between Python 2.x and Python 3.x?"

The latest version of Python 3.12.0 (as of publication). You can still download Python 2.7.17 but it's important that you note that this version is no longer supported. This means that no new bug reports, fixes, or changes are available for Python 2.x and haven't been since the 1st of January 2020.

For the purposes of this book, we will be using Python 3.x.

So why does version 2.x even exist? Well, the simple answer is code migration. The difference between version 2.x and version 3.x means that programs and scripts that were used in the earlier version now need to be recoded so that they're compatible with the new version of Python.

When dealing with smaller programs that use version 2.x, code migration is pretty simple and easy. Having said that, more complex programs that contain thousands of lines of coding can become a much bigger headache. The obstacle between these two program versions comes with the changes to the behavior and the syntax of the programming languages.

For example, if you divide 3 and 2 using the '/' operator in Python 2.x, you will receive an output of 1. If you divide the same numbers with the same operator in Python 3.x, you will receive an output of 1.5.

Version 3.x is undeniably more efficient but the old versions of Python are still needed purely because of the issues mentioned above. Larger programs that were written in version 2's runtime environment are just too tedious to migrate over and so developers haven't bothered to make the transition. If you plan on working on existing programs, then we would suggest version 2.x but a friendly reminder that this book and the exercises in it will focus on version 3.x.

Installing the Interpreter

Python requires a runtime environment and command line interpreter. When you download Python from the official Python site your program will contain both of these. Installing the program on Mac and Windows is particularly easy.

All you need to do is head to the website, www.python.org (Python), and select downloads from the menu bar.

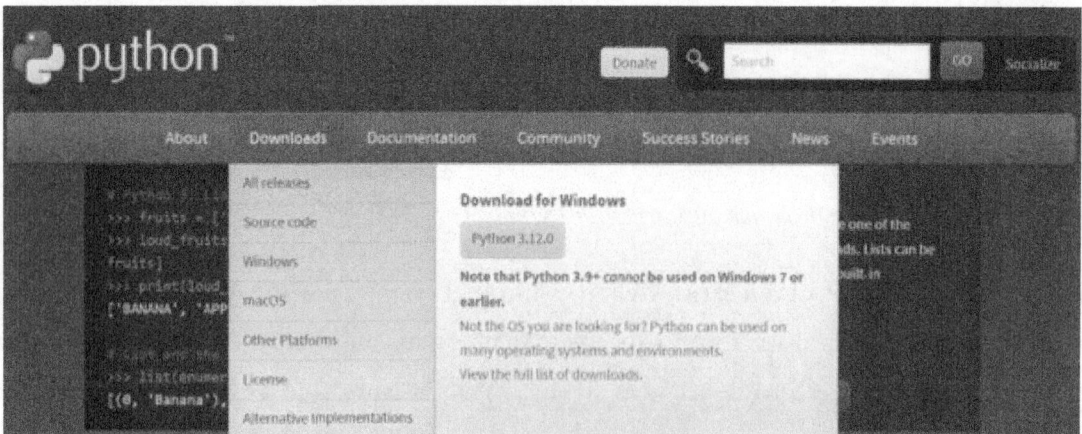

Here, you'll find a list of platforms as well as the latest version of Python, free to download.

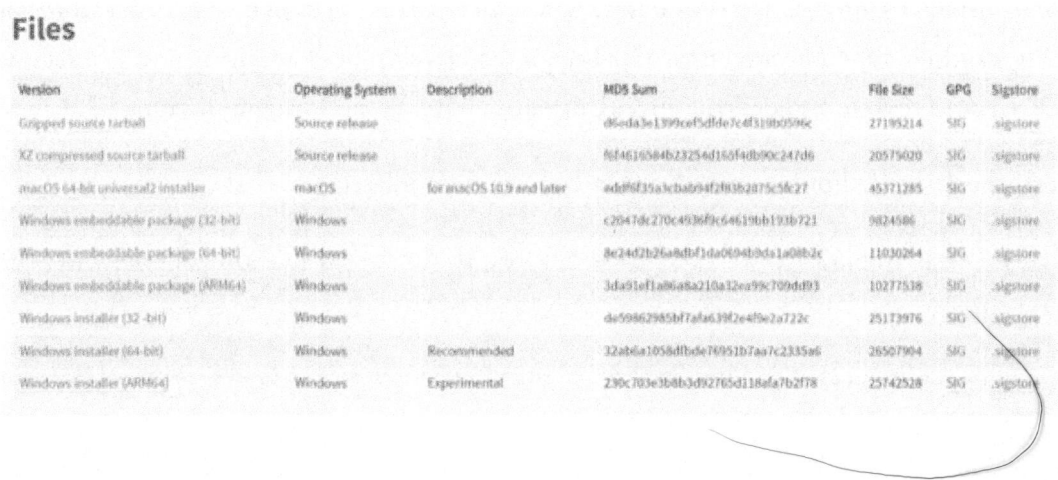

You will need to follow a few simple step-by-step instructions as you install your program. These have been screenshotted for you using a Windows operating system.

If you choose a custom installation, you will need to select the packages and features you want installed in your system so make sure you check the following. Alternatively, you can choose to install by selecting the "Recommended" option.

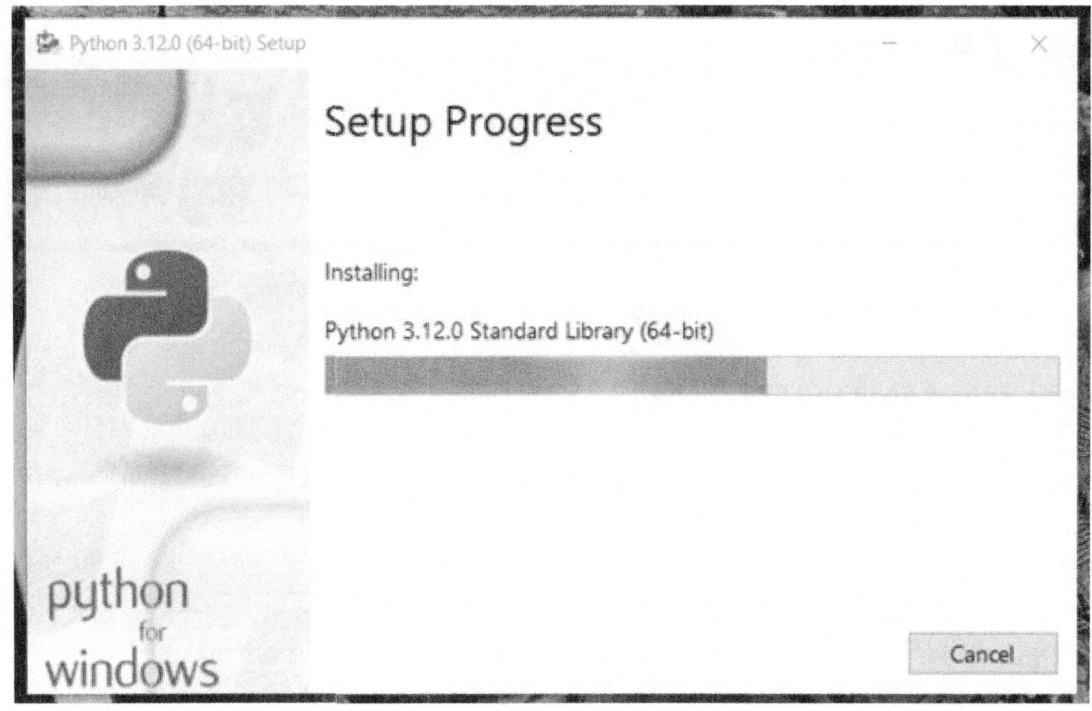

Tcl/tk installs TkInter. This is the Graphic User Interface (GUI) toolkit you need if you plan to create windows for your programs. The Integrated Development and Learning Environment (IDLE) both require and depend on TkInter since it is a Python program with a GUI.

Next, check the Python test suite feature. You will need it later.

Finally, PIP is an optional feature that allows you to download Python packages later on in your journey.

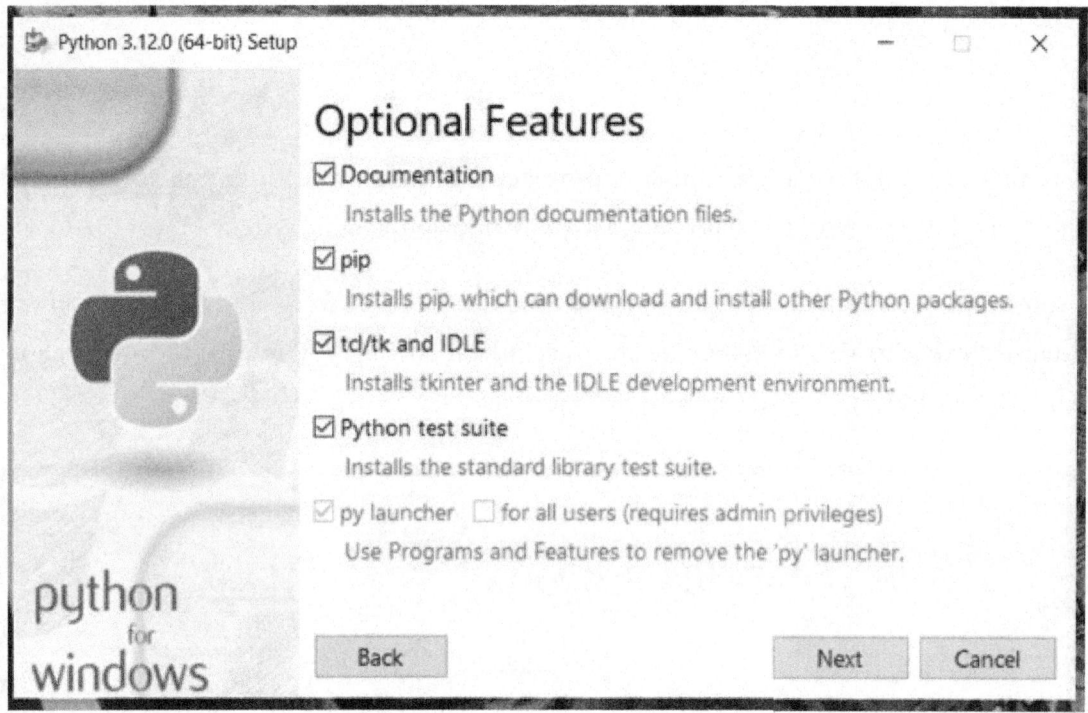

Using Python Shell and IDLE

There are two ways to run a Python program. These are by using its runtime environment or using the command line interpreter.

The command line interpreter has two forms. The first one is the regular Python shell and the second one is IDLE or Integrated Development and Learning Environment.

The regular Python shell uses the familiar command line interface (CLI) or terminal look.

IDLE is a Python program encased in a regular graphical user interface (GUI) window. IDLE is full of easy-to-access menu, customization options, and GUI functions while the Python shell is devoid of those and only offers a command prompt (i.e. the input field in a text-based user interface screen).

One of the beneficial functions of IDLE is its syntax highlighting. The syntax highlighting function makes it easier for programmers or scripters to identify between keywords, operators, variables, and numeric literals.

Also, you can customize the highlight color and the font properties displayed on IDLE. With the shell, you only get a monospaced font, white font color, and black background.

All of the examples in this book are written in the Python shell. However, it is okay for you to write using IDLE. It is suited for beginners since they do not need to worry about indentation and code management. Not to mention that the syntax highlighting is truly beneficial.

Writing Your First Program

Okay, so to get started, it's a tradition for new programmers to begin with the "Hello World" program.

- Open Python by finding it in your "Start" menu.

- Create a new file by navigating to "File," and then "New File."

- Save this file as "Hello World."

- Write this line.

- Type print("Hello World!")

- Run the module by selecting "Run" or pressing F5.

```
File  Edit  Format  Run  Options  Window  Help
print ("Hello World!")
```

- Hit Enter on your keyboard.

- Python will respond with: Hello World!

```
IDLE Shell 3.12.0                                          —   □   ×
File Edit Shell Debug Options Window Help
    Python 3.12.0 (tags/v3.12.0:0fb18b0, Oct  2 2023, 13:03:39) [MSC v.1935 64 bit (
    AMD64)] on win32
    Type "help", "copyright", "credits" or "license()" for more information.
>>>
    = RESTART: C:/Users/.     `AppData/Local/Programs/Python/Python312/Hello World.py
    Hello World!
>>>
                                                                          Ln: 6 Col: 0
```

Shell, IDLE, and Scripts Syntax

Like every other human language, programming languages have grammar and writing rules. These are called syntax and these rules in programming languages are extremely strict but fairly simple.

Humans have an innate ability to interpret and understand context when foreigners are speaking their language. Computers, on the other hand, lack intuition and cognitive abilities. They need proper and precise statements for them to know exactly what you need so when you make a syntax error, your entire program can stop functioning or your computer may simply stop your program from running.

When you typed your Hello World program, you would have noticed that Shell and IDLE have a prompt that looks like this: >>>

Generally, when you start writing a code, you'll do so after this prompt. Having said that, when you write code in a file like py, script, or module, you do not need to write after the prompt.

Indentation

While you're programming, you'll come across or will create code blocks. A code block is a piece of Python's program text. This is called a statement and can be executed as a unit, like a module, a class definition, or a function body.

These often end with a colon (:).

Indentations are done with four spaces by default but you can do away with any number of spaces, as long as the code block has a uniform number of spaces before each statement.

Let's look at an example.

- Go ahead and open the IDLE Shell.
- You'll see your three greater than signs which means Python is ready for your Python command (>>>)
- Type in the following code,
  - print('Welcome to Python')
- Next, click enter.

```
IDLE Shell 3.12.0
File Edit Shell Debug Options Window Help
Python 3.12.0 (tags/v3.12.0:0fb18b0, Oct  2 2023, 13:03:39) [MSC v.1935 64 bit (
AMD64)] on win32
Type "help", "copyright", "credits" or "license()" for more information.
>>> print('Welcome to Python')
Welcome to Python
>>>
```

This is pretty much the same as your Hello World code. Right?

Let's expand upon this.

- Without clearing your code, type the following

    ○ Greeting='Welcome to Python'

    ○ Enter

- print(Greeting)

Python will run your code as follows

```
Python 3.12.0 (tags/v3.12.0:0fb18b0, Oct  2 2023, 13:03:39) [MSC v.1935 64 bit (AMD64)] on win32
Type "help", "copyright", "credits" or "license()" for more information.
>>> print('Welcome to Python')
Welcome to Python
>>> Greeting='Welcome to Python'
>>> print(Greeting)
Welcome to Python
>>>
```

Indentation Prompt

While using the Python Shell, it will tell you when to indent by using the prompt (...) or by bringing up a list of suggested prompts.

Give it a try by typing in the following,

- x=1

- Press Enter

- print (

Python will bring up a list of suggested prompts as follows

```
Python 3.12.0 (tags/v3.12.0:0fb18b0, Oct  2 2023, 13:03:39) [MSC v.1935 64 bit (AMD64)] on win32
Type "help", "copyright", "credits" or "license()" for more information.
>>> x=1
>>> print(
        (*args, sep=' ', end='\n', file=None, flush=False)
        Prints the values to a stream, or to sys.stdout by default.
```

- Go ahead and complete your code

- print (x)

In IDLE your indentation will be automatic. To escape an indentation or code block, all you need to do is press Enter or go to the next line.

Let's try another fun code.

- y=2

- Enter

- print ('nothing to see here!')

- Enter

Your code will return with nothing to see here!

Simple, right?

Python Shell Navigation

While in Python Shell, you cannot interact with your mouse. Your cursor will be limited to the window's context menu, window commands, and scrolling functions. When copying and pasting, you need to use the window's context menu.

Most of the navigation you do in the shell is moving the navigation caret (the blinking white underscore). You can, however, move it using the navigation keys (left and right arrow keys, PgUp, PgDn, Home, End, and so on).

IDLE Navigation

The IDLE window is just like a regular GUI window. It contains a menu bar where you can access most of IDLE's functions and use the mouse directly on IDLE's work area like you would when using a regular word processing program.

Unlike Shell, IDLE provides a lot more helpful features that can assist you while you are programming. When it comes to advanced Python programming, IDLE is the main tool used to develop Python programs. Having said that, you're not limited to using it and you can actually use other development environments or word processors to create your programming scripts.

Troubleshooting Installation Issues

The first thing you're going to want to make sure of is that you're downloading your installation file directly from the Python website.

www.python.org

Always choose the correct installation file for your operating system by following the steps in the *Installing the Interpreter* section of this chapter.

Make sure that you're not installing a version of Python that isn't supported by your operating system. For example, PCs still running Windows XP will not be able to support the latest version of Python. Also, keep in mind that there are two versions of each release for Windows operating systems. These are 32 or 64-bit. If you're not sure what version of Windows you have, go ahead and install the 32-bit version as the installer will recommend which version to install.

For Linux, going to the Python website to download the installation file is not necessary. Linux's distribution operating system's package manager can be used. Having said that, it's always a good idea to check the website if you do not see Python on your computer.

Make sure you have at least 100MB of free disk space before installing Python. Take note of where your program is installed.

Should you not be able to find your Python Shell, or the installation doesn't create shortcuts for you, you can create them by

- right-clicking Python in your search bar
- Selecting Open file location

- Selecting Python IDLE from your list

- And following the usual steps to pin to task and start bars

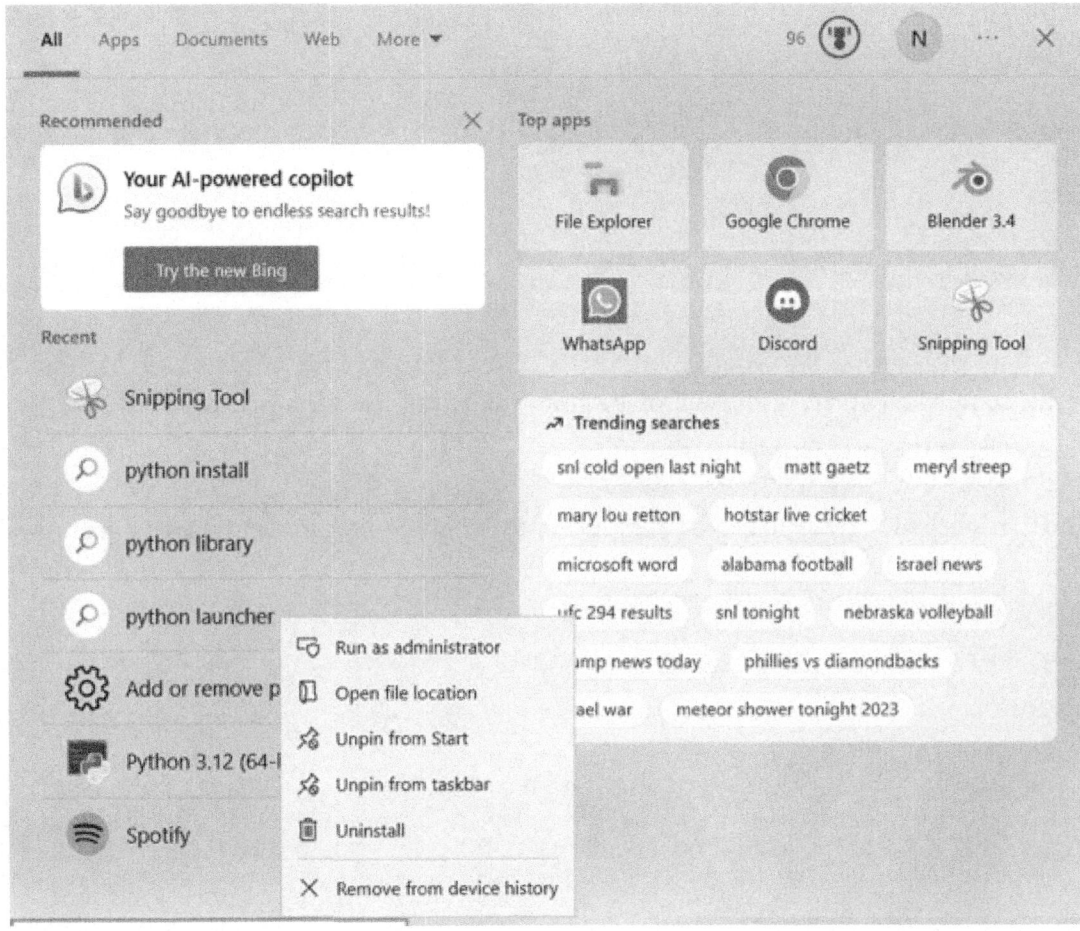

Name	Date modified	Type	Size
IDLE (Python 3.12 64-bit)	10/22/2023 3:51 PM	Shortcut	3 KB
Python 3.12 (64-bit)	10/20/2023 4:50 PM	Shortcut	2 KB
Python 3.12 Manuals (64-bit)	10/20/2023 4:50 PM	Shortcut	2 KB
Python 3.12 Module Docs (64-bit)	10/20/2023 4:50 PM	Shortcut	3 KB

If all else fails, complete a reinstall of Python, following the prompts to install additional features from the installation library.

And that's it, you're ready to begin your journey to programming greatness, so let's get on with it.

CHAPTER 3

Variables and Operators in Python

As you expand upon your knowledge of Python, you're going to need to pick up some new lingo. In this chapter, the new words for the day will be variables and operators.

A variable is another name for a Python identifier. It is used to imply a memory zone of a machine or device. Now, in Python, you don't decide these kinds of factors as the programming language infers it and is astute enough to sort variables. In other words, variables in Python are memory locations that have different data types like integers or characters. These variables are changeable and manipulable because they are a set of operations.

For variables to work, they require a letter or an underscore to initialize. We suggest using lower-case letters as variable names. We'll dive into operators a little later in this chapter, for now, let's take a deeper look at Python variables.

Creating Variables

The first thing you need to know is that Python has no command for declaring a variable. This is because a variable is created from the moment you first assign a value to it.

This means you do not need to declare your variable with any particular type, and can even change the type after it has been set. Neat, right?

Let's try it out.

Open Python and type in the following code.

```
x = 5
y = 'John'
print(x)
print(y)
```

Remember to press enter after each line of code!

```
IDLE Shell 3.12.0
File Edit Shell Debug Options Window Help
    Python 3.12.0 (tags/v3.12.0:0fb18b0, Oct  2 2023, 13:03:39) [MSC v.1935 64 bit (
    AMD64)] on win32
    Type "help", "copyright", "credits" or "license()" for more information.
>>> x=5
>>> y='John'
>>> print(x)
    5
>>> print(y)
    John
>>>
```

Remember we said that you do not need to declare your variable with any particular type?

Let's try it out by entering the following code.

- x=7

- x='Jane'

- print(x)

What is your end result?

```
Python 3.12.0 (tags/v3.12.0:0fb18b0, Oct  2 2023, 13:03:39) [MSC v.1935 64 bit (AMD64)] on win32
Type "help", "copyright", "credits" or "license()" for more information.
>>> x=7
>>> x='Jane'
>>> print(x)
Jane
>>>
```

In this example, x is of type integer. x='Jane' means x is now of type built-in string.

You can specify the data type of a variable by casting but we'll get to that a little later in this book. For now, let's look at naming of variables or identifiers.

The Naming of Variables or Identifiers

Factors are the characteristics of names and a variable is used to store the actual numbers and whole numbers being used in your program. To make this easier to understand, let's look at some Python standards when naming a variable.

- The essential character of any identifier must be a letter "altogether," or an underscore.

- Each of the characters besides the essential characters may contain lowercase letters, capital letters, underscores, or digits from 0 to 9.

- A variable name cannot contain an empty zone or any special character. This includes !, @, #, %, $, and so on.

- Variable names cannot resemble any of Python's own syntax catchphrases.

- Variables are case-sensitive. Inputting variable, Variable, and VARIABLE are all considered different variables in Python.

```
IDLE Shell 3.12.0                                          —   □   ×
File Edit Shell Debug Options Window Help
    Python 3.12.0 (tags/v3.12.0:0fb18b0, Oct  2 2023, 13:03:39) [MSC v.1935 64 bit (
    AMD64)] on win32
    Type "help", "copyright", "credits" or "license()" for more information.
>>> variable=10
>>> Variable=20
>>> VARIABLE=30
>>> print(variable)
    10
>>> print(Variable)
    20
>>> print(VARIABLE)
    30
>>> print(vAriable)
    Traceback (most recent call last):
      File "<pyshell#6>", line 1, in <module>
        print(vAriable)
    NameError: name 'vAriable' is not defined. Did you mean: 'variable'?
>>>
                                                              Ln: 17  Col: 0
```

Multiple Assignments

When using Python, you have the ability to assign values to multiple variables in a single statement. This is commonly referred to as multiple assignments. What this feature does is allow you to assign the same value to multiple variables at once. Alternatively, you can assign different values to multiple variables at different times.

Let's take a look at this in action.

Open Python and enter the following code:

- x=y=z=10

- Hit Enter

In this example, x, y, and z have all been assigned the value 10. This means entering

- print(x)

Will return the same value of 10 as if you entered print y, or print z.

```
IDLE Shell 3.12.0
File Edit Shell Debug Options Window Help
    Python 3.12.0 (tags/v3.12.0:0fb18b0, Oct  2 2023, 13:03:39) [MSC v.1935 64 bit (
    AMD64)] on win32
    Type "help", "copyright", "credits" or "license()" for more information.
>>> x=y=z=10
>>> print(x)
    10
>>> print(y)
    10
>>> print(z)
    10
>>> 
```

Now let's try the following code.

- a=5

- b=7

- c='hello'

Here, we're assigning the values 5 to letter a, 7 to letter b, and the string 'hello' to variable c.

```
IDLE Shell 3.12.0                                          —    □    ×
File Edit Shell Debug Options Window Help
    Python 3.12.0 (tags/v3.12.0:0fb18b0, Oct  2 2023, 13:03:39) [MSC v.1935 64 bit (
    AMD64)] on win32
    Type "help", "copyright", "credits" or "license()" for more information.
>>> a=5
>>> b=7
>>> c='hello'
>>> print(a)
    5
>>> print(b)
    7
>>> print(c)
    hello
>>> print(a,b,c)
    5 7 hello
>>> |
```

This allows for flexibility in how you assign value to variables when using Python.

Operators in Python

Python operators are symbols that allow you to perform certain actions or calculations. An easy way to think of operators is as tools that have been borrowed from other sciences. For example, + is an operator in Python that is used to add two or more numbers and would be borrowed from mathematics.

Each of Python's operators is similar to function shortcuts that are represented by symbols. They help your program to perform different functions with numbers or values. These operators are the building blocks of your program and are needed to perform tasks within the Python language.

Python has various operators, including

- Arithmetic operators
- Assignment operators
- Comparison operators
- Logical operators
- Identity operators
- Membership operators
- Bitwise operators

Let's break each of these down with an example. Your final exercise in this chapter will revolve around arithmetic operators, so pay attention and experiment until you get it right.

Arithmetic Operators

With arithmetic operators you have two things called operands that you're going to work with. You can use an operator to perform an action on these operands and the action you've taken will result in a specific and definite value. In other words, your operator helps you to combine or manipulate the operands to produce a clear and expected outcome.

Let's break it down further. Let's say you have the operands of 3 and 6 and you use the operator +. The action performed in addition and the specific value or outcome you'll get is 9.

The operator + helped you combine and manipulate your operands 3 and 6 to produce an outcome that is clear and specific.

Arithmetic operators include

- Addition— +
- Subtraction— -
- Division— /
- Multiplication— *
- Remainder— %

Let's give it a try using your Python coding skills.

Open Python and enter the following code.

- result=6+3
- print(result)

```
IDLE Shell 3.12.0
File Edit Shell Debug Options Window Help
    Python 3.12.0 (tags/v3.12.0:0fb18b0, Oct  2 2023, 13:03:39) [MSC v.1935 64 bit (
    AMD64)] on win32
    Type "help", "copyright", "credits" or "license()" for more information.
>>> result=6+3
>>> print(result)
    9
>>>
```

We'll try something a little more complex.

- n,v=25,69

- n+v

Remember to hit enter!

What did your console print after entering n+v?

If it returned 94; Well done!

```
Python 3.12.0 (tags/v3.12.0:0fb18b0, Oct  2 2023, 13:03:39) [MSC v.1935 64 bit (AMD64)] on win32
Type "help", "copyright", "credits" or "license()" for more information.
>>> n,v=25,69
>>> n+v
94
>>> 
```

You can use any mathematical operator in this way with as many operands as you like. For example,

- a,b,c,d=25,25,50,50

- a+b+c-d

```
IDLE Shell 3.12.0                                    —  □  ×
File Edit Shell Debug Options Window Help
    Python 3.12.0 (tags/v3.12.0:0fb18b0, Oct  2 2023, 13:03:39) [MSC v.1935 64 bit (
    AMD64)] on win32
    Type "help", "copyright", "credits" or "license()" for more information.
>>> a,b,c,d=25,25,50,50
>>> a+b+c-d
    50
>>>
```

A Word on Remainder Operators

The remainder operator is denoted by the % sign and calculates what is left over when you divide one number by another. If your division is perfect and there is no remainder, the output result will be 0 (zero). If, however, there is a remainder, the result will be reflected as only the remainder.

If we look at the following example,

- a,b=6,3

- a%b

This will return a result of 0 (zero) as 6 is divisible by 3 perfectly.

If, however, your code were,

- a,b=6,4

- a%b

The result would be 2.

```
Python 3.12.0 (tags/v3.12.0:0fb18b0, Oct  2 2023, 13:03:39) [MSC v.1935 64 bit (
AMD64)] on win32
Type "help", "copyright", "credits" or "license()" for more information.
>>> a,b=6,3
>>> a%b
0
>>> a,b=6,4
>>> 6%4
2
>>>
```

Assignment Operators

Assignment operators are used to assign values to variables when using Python. They essentially combine the assignment operation with another operation like addition, subtraction, multiplication, and so on, and update the value of the variable.

Using assignment operators makes it far more convenient to perform calculations and update variables in a single step.

The = sign is the simplest assignment operator. It assigns the value on the right to the variable on the left.

- x = 5— Assigns the value 5 to the variable x

Add and assign += adds the value on the right to the variable on the left.

- x = 5

- x += 3— Adds 3 to x and assigns the result to x.

- x is now 8

Subtract and assign -= subtracts the value on the right from the variable on the left.

- x = 10

- x -= 2— Subtracts 2 from x and assigns the result to x.

- x is now 8

Multiply and assign *= multiplies the variable on the left by the value on the right.

- x = 4

- x *= 3— Multiplies x by 3 and assigns the result to x.

- x is now 12

Divide and assign /= divides the variable on the left by the value on the right.

- x = 20

- x /= 4— Divides x by 4 and assigns the result to x

- x is now 5.0 (floating-point result)

Floor division and assign //= performs floor division on the variable on the left by the value on the right.

- x = 21
- x //= 4— Floor divides x by 4 and assigns the result to x
- x is now 5

Modulus and assign %= calculates the remainder when the variable on the left is divided by the value on the right.

- x = 17
- x %= 5— Calculates the remainder of x divided by 5 and assigns it to x
- x is now 2

What makes assignment operators so handy is that they update variables with the results of various calculations. This makes your code more readable and concise.

Comparison Operators

In Python, comparison operators are used to compare two operands and return a TRUE or FALSE outcome. This is called a Boolean type.

Comparison operators can be

- == (true: this operator is used if the values are logically equal and true).
- != (true: used when values are true but unequal).
- <= (true: used when the first operand is smaller than or equal to the second operand).
- >= (true: used when the first operand is greater than or equal to the second operand).
- <>(true: this operator is used if the values are not equal).
- > (true: used when the first operand is greater than the second).

- < (true: used when the first operand is less than the second).

Let's take a look at some practical examples of comparison operators. Open up Python and enter the following code,

- 5 == 5

- Enter

Python will return with True

Now enter

- 5==3

- Enter

Python will return with False

```
IDLE Shell 3.12.0
File Edit Shell Debug Options Window Help
    Python 3.12.0 (tags/v3.12.0:0fb18b0, Oct  2 2023, 13:03:39) [MSC v.1935 64 bit (
    AMD64)] on win32
    Type "help", "copyright", "credits" or "license()" for more information.
>>> 5==5
    True
>>> 5==3
    False
>>>
```

Let's try another one. Enter the code,

- 5 >= 5

- Enter

Python returns with True.

Now enter,

- 8>=11

- Enter

Python returns with False.

```
Python 3.12.0 (tags/v3.12.0:0fb18b0, Oct  2 2023, 13:03:39) [MSC v.1935 64 bit (AMD64)] on win32
Type "help", "copyright", "credits" or "license()" for more information.
>>> 5>=5
True
>>> 8>=11
False
>>> 
```

Assignment Operators

An assignment operator is used to assign values to variables by combining the assignment operation with another operation like addition, subtraction, multiplication, and so on. This updates the value of a variable to the result of the combined operation.

= assigns a value to a variable.

- Example: x =3— x now equals to 3

+= adds a value to the current value of a variable and assigns the result to the variable.

- Example: x=3
- x+=5— adds 5 to x and assigns the result to x. Therefore, x is now 8.

-= subtracts a value from the current value of a variable and assigns the result to the variable.

- Example: x=3
- x-=1— subtracts 1 from x and assigns the result to x. Therefore, x is now 2.

*= multiplies a value to the current value of a variable and assigns the result to the variable.

- Example: x=3
- x*=5— multiples 5 by x and assigns the result to x. Therefore, x is now 15.

/= divides a value of the current value of a variable and assigns the result to the variable.

- Example: x=6
- x/=2— divides 6 by 2 and assigns the result to x. Therefore, x is now 3.

%= calculates the remainder of dividing a variable by a specific value and assigns the remainder to the variable.

- Example: x=6
- x%=4— calculates the remainder as 2 and assigns the result to x. Therefore, x is now 2.

Remember that %= requires non-perfect division. Perfection division will result in 0 being assigned.

Check out the picture below for a full list of the equations above.

```
Python 3.12.0 (tags/v3.12.0:0fb18b0, Oct  2 2023, 13:03:39) [MSC v.1935 64 bit (AMD64)] on win32
Type "help", "copyright", "credits" or "license()" for more information.
>>> x=3
>>> print(x)
3
>>> x=3
>>> x+=5
>>> print(x)
8
>>> x=3
>>> x-=1
>>> print(x)
2
>>> x=3
>>> x*=5
>>> print(x)
15
>>> x=6
>>> x/=2
>>> print(x)
3.0
>>> x=6
>>> x%=4
>>> print(x)
2
>>> x=6
>>> x%=3
>>> print(x)
0
>>>
```

Logical Operators

In Python, logical operators are used to perform logical operations on Boolean values. These allow you to combine multiple conditions that make decisions based on the results of these combinations.

This is a mouthful, I know, so let's look at a real-life example. Let's say you are sitting at home and someone calls to ask you, "Are you at home?" You have a choice based on logical true or false data and this is "Yes, I am home," or "No, I am not home." Now logical data always only has two choices, true or false. Because of this, you can't input complex conditions that could have various outputs. You can only use logical operators to evaluate the expressions and obtain a *specific* decision.

As such, logical operators are helpful when writing any logic reasonably but only if that logic is *reasonable*. Look at the list of logical operators below, along with a brief description for a better understanding.

The And Operator

The And operator returns True if both conditions on its left and right sides are True. Conversely, if either or both conditions are *False*, the result is *False*.

```
IDLE Shell 3.12.0                                              —    □    ×
File  Edit  Shell  Debug  Options  Window  Help
    Python 3.12.0 (tags/v3.12.0:0fb18b0, Oct  2 2023, 13:03:39) [MSC v.1935 64 bit (
    AMD64)] on win32
    Type "help", "copyright", "credits" or "license()" for more information.
>>> x=True
>>> y=True
>>> result=x and y
>>> result
    True
>>> 
                                                                    Ln: 8  Col: 0
```

The Or Operator

The *Or* operator returns true if at least one of the conditions on the left or right sides are *True*. If, however, both conditions are *False*, the result will be *False*.

```
Python 3.12.0 (tags/v3.12.0:0fb18b0, Oct  2 2023, 13:03:39) [MSC v.1935 64 bit (AMD64)] on win32
Type "help", "copyright", "credits" or "license()" for more information.
>>> x=True
>>> y=False
>>> result=x or y
>>> result
True
>>>
```

The Not Operator

The *Not* operator works on a single condition. This means it is a unary operator and it reverses the condition. In other words, if the condition is *True*, *Not* makes it *False* and vice versa.

```
IDLE Shell 3.12.0                                           —    □    ×
File Edit Shell Debug Options Window Help
    Python 3.12.0 (tags/v3.12.0:0fb18b0, Oct  2 2023, 13:03:39) [MSC v.1935 64 bit (
    AMD64)] on win32
    Type "help", "copyright", "credits" or "license()" for more information.
>>> x=True
>>> result=not x
>>> result
    False
>>>
```

The Identity Operator

We're almost nearing the end of this chapter, hang tight future programmer extraordinaire!

Our next operators are Identity operators. These are used to determine if two variables or objects are referring to the same memory location. Alternatively, it may be used to determine if two variables or objects have the same identity. There are two primary identity operators, these being *is* and *is not*.

is Operator

The *is* operator checks if two variables or objects are referencing the same memory location. If they do, Python returns *True* and if they don't, it returns *False*.

```
Python 3.12.0 (tags/v3.12.0:0fb18b0, Oct  2 2023, 13:03:39) [MSC v.1935 64 bit (AMD64)] on win32
Type "help", "copyright", "credits" or "license()" for more information.
>>> x=(1,2,3)
>>> y=x
>>> result=x is y
>>> result
True
>>> 
```

is not Operator

The *is not* operator checks if two variables or objects do not reference the same memory location. If these do not reference the same memory, Python returns *True*. If they do reference the same memory, it returns *False*.

```
Python 3.12.0 (tags/v3.12.0:0fb18b0, Oct  2 2023, 13:03:39) [MSC v.1935 64 bit (AMD64)] on win32
Type "help", "copyright", "credits" or "license()" for more information.
>>> x=(1,2,3)
>>> y=x
>>> result=x is y
>>> result
True
>>> x=(4,5,6)
>>> y=(4,5,6)
>>> result=x is not y
>>> result
True
>>>
```

Membership Operators

Membership operators are used to test if a specific value is present in a sequence. This could be a string, list, tuple, or dictionary (don't worry, we'll get to this later in this book). In Python, there are two main membership operators, the in operator and the not operator.

in Operator

The *in* operator checks if a specified value exists in a particular sequence. If the value is found, Python returns *True* and if it is not found, it returns *False*.

```
Python 3.12.0 (tags/v3.12.0:0fb18b0, Oct  2 2023, 13:03:39) [MSC v.1935 64 bit (AMD64)] on win32
Type "help", "copyright", "credits" or "license()" for more information.
>>> house=('walls', 'floors', 'windows')
>>> result='walls'in house
>>> result
True
>>> house=('walls', 'floors', 'windows')
>>> result='doors'in house
>>> result
False
>>>
```

not in Operator

The *not in* operator checks if a specified value does not exist in a sequence. If the value is not found, Python returns with *True* and if it is found, it returns *False*.

```
IDLE Shell 3.12.0                                    —    □    ×
File Edit Shell Debug Options Window Help
    Python 3.12.0 (tags/v3.12.0:0fb18b0, Oct  2 2023, 13:03:39) [MSC v.1935 64 bit (
    AMD64)] on win32
    Type "help", "copyright", "credits" or "license()" for more information.
>>> text='hello world'
>>> result='goodbye world' not in text
>>> result
    True
>>> text='hello world'
>>> result='hello world' not in text
>>> result
    False
>>>
```

Bitwise Operators

The final operator you'll learn about is the Bitwise operator. These operators are used to perform operations on individual bits of binary numbers. We won't go into too much detail here as bitwise operators are typically used in very low-level programming like when you're working with hardware, or optimizing algorithms.

There are six bitwise operators, namely

AND '&'— Performs a bitwise AND operation on each pair of corresponding bits in two binary numbers.

OR '|'— Performs a bitwise OR operation on each pair of corresponding bits in two binary numbers.

XOR '^'— Performs a bitwise XOR (exclusive OR) operation on each pair of corresponding bits in two binary numbers.

NOT '~'— Performs a bitwise NOT operation on each bit in a binary number.

Left shift '<<'— Shifts the bits of a binary number to the left by a specified number of positions.

Right shift '>>'— Shifts the bits of a binary number to the right by a specified number of positions.

Because you'll probably not be using bitwise operators for general Python programming, it's best to take a separate course that focuses on programming hardware.

And, you've reached the end of this chapter! Before moving on to the next chapter, let's put everything you've learned into action.

Foundational Exercise for Operators

It's time to test your knowledge for Chapter 3, here is your exercise!

Create a Python program that calculates and prints the area of an equilateral triangle.

Exercise hints:

- The formula to calculate the area of a triangle is Area = (1/2) * Base * Height

- Enter the base of the triangle at 4 inches (4.0).

- Enter the height of the triangle at 4 inches (4.0).

- Calculate the area using the formula above.

- Don't forget to display (print) your result!

Open Python and give it a try.

The solution is on the next page.

```
Python 3.12.0 (tags/v3.12.0:0fb18b0, Oct  2 2023, 13:03:39) [MSC v.1935 64 bit (AMD64)] on win32
Type "help", "copyright", "credits" or "license()" for more information.
>>> base=4.0
>>> height=4.0
>>> area=(1/2)*base*height
>>> print('The area of the triangle with base', base, 'inches and height', height, 'inches is', area, 'square inches.')
The area of the triangle with base 4.0 inches and height 4.0 inches is 8.0 square inches.
>>>
```

CHAPTER 4

Python Data Types

When it comes to dealing with programming and technology, data is at the core of everything you're doing. The definition of data is pretty broad and can be something as simple as a number or text message to something far more complex like databases and lists of items.

If you're going to work effectively in Python, you're going to need to understand each of these common data types—these are classifications that specify which type of value a variable can hold. Because Python is typed dynamically, you don't need to declare the data type of a variable explicitly. Python does this for you, figuring out the data type of a variable based on the value assigned to it.

How does Python do this?

Well, it provides users with a variety of built-in data types that can handle different types of data. These include

Integers (int)

Floating-point numbers (float)

Strings (str)

Boolean (bool)

Tuples

Dictionaries (dict)

Sets

NoneType (None)

In this chapter, we're going to deal with the basics, moving onto harder data types from Chapter 6 onward. But first, let's chat about Python labels.

Labels

When you write code, you're naming variables and objects appropriately so that others can understand what you are looking at and so you know what *you're* looking at immediately. Labels, or identifiers, are words that represent something in a way that makes the code far easier to read. Here's an example. Let's say you're talking about a can of soda in code. Instead of naming this can of soda "variable1," which would require you to go through your notes to identify it, you could name it "soda."

This saves you a whole lot of time!

There are some dos and don'ts when it comes to labels. For example, you wouldn't use variations of the same name over and over again as this would be confusing for you and possibly Python. Another rule is that you cannot use words that are part of Python's own library of keywords. These words are reserved for different commands within the program itself. These include words like *True, False, import, print, result,* and so on.

Applying Variables

When using Python, a variable definition is handled in two separate steps. The first of these steps is called initialization. This refers to assigning, or determining the container that is identified via a label.

The second step involves assignment. This means you attach a value to your variable and this determines the type of data it holds. While these two steps are defined separately, they actually happen at the same time and with the same process. As such, you probably won't even notice it.

You take the two steps mentioned above with the equal (=) operator. This is called a statement—more specifically, an assignment statement—but you already knew that if you were paying attention in Chapter 3!

> ***Pro Tip: When coding, you should always keep your statements in proper order.***

Always remember that Python processes code by analyzing it from the top down before starting over. Also, keep in mind that Python has a feature called dynamic typing. This means it can automatically determine the kind of variable being dealt with. In other words, if you apply an integer to a variable, Python knows it's an integer data type.

This is great, but there is one disadvantage to dynamic typing—you may accidentally create a variable when you don't need it, or assign the wrong data type to your variable. You need to pay attention to all the variables you have created which can be a lot.

An easy way around this is to declare all of your variables at the beginning of your programming project. The beauty of Python is that the program isn't affected by simple assignments. The reason for this is that is because you're not instructing the interpreter to perform an operation. In other words, if you say 'a is equal to 5' then there's nothing else to input.

This, of course, doesn't mean you have to have all your variables figured out before you begin programming. It just means you can start your program by declaring whatever you need to and then add more later, should you have to.

Have you got the hang of applying variables? If not, I'd suggest going back and recapping Chapter 3. If you've got it, let's move on to our next section.

Strings

Along with numbers, strings are the most basic data type data types when it comes to Python. In the examples throughout the previous chapters, you've already used strings—the line of text you input and print is this string. To put it simply, strings are the sets of characters that you type and which are defined between quotation marks.

Strings contain numbers and punctuation marks, even if these are considered text, but numbers alone, and when defined by quotation marks, are classified under their own data types, like integers and floats.

Here's an example to simplify this concept, open up Python and type in the following,

- charRace='human'

- charGender='male'

- print=(carRace,charGender)

```
Python 3.12.0 (tags/v3.12.0:0fb18b0, Oct  2 2023, 13:03:39) [MSC v.1935 64 bit (AMD64)] on win32
Type "help", "copyright", "credits" or "license()" for more information.
>>> charRace='human'
>>> charGender='male'
>>> print(charRace,charGender)
human male
>>>
```

In the code above, there are two variables, and these two variables contain their own string. By separating the variables with commas when writing your print statement, both are printed. There are multiple ways you can do this, but using commas is the easiest way because it ensures you have a clear separator and can find mistakes in your code.

Another issue with not using commas as separators is that if you don't want to use variables but you do need to concatenate strings, your text could change. For example, if you were to input print("school""teacher") and wanted the outcome schoolteacher that would be fine. However, if you were looking to print, school teacher, the only way to achieve your desired outcome would be to separate your variables.

There is one other way to separate variables when they contain their own string, and you've already practiced this as well. This is by separating your code along different lines.

For example,

x='human'

y='male'

x+y

Here you've used a mathematical operator combined with string variables but again, your output is not going to be exactly what you want. Right? Unless your desired outcome was humanmale without a white space. Besides this undesired outcome, using mathematical operations requires processing power. In essence, you're telling Python to use more power from your computer to perform an operation that probably won't produce the exact outcome you're after.

As such, it's a good idea to stick with tried and true, power-saving coding techniques that help keep your code simple and easy to read.

Let's test your string knowledge. Write a program that has an outcome of men aged 25 to 35 for yyy's social media demographic and women aged 19 to 24 for yyy social media demographic.

Print the full string to display only men and a separate print of the full string to display only women demographics.

Finally, print yyy social media's full demographic of both women and men.

I'll give you a minute... The solution is on the next page.

```
Python 3.12.0 (tags/v3.12.0:0fb18b0, Oct  2 2023, 13:03:39) [MSC v.1935 64 bit (
AMD64)] on win32
Type "help", "copyright", "credits" or "license()" for more information.
>>> company=('yyy social media')
>>> demographic=('male', 'age 25 to 35')
>>> altdemographic=('female', 'age 19 to 24')
>>> print(company, demographic)
yyy social media ('male', 'age 25 to 35')
>>> print(company,altdemographic)
yyy social media ('female', 'age 19 to 24')
>>> print(company,demographic,altdemographic)
yyy social media ('male', 'age 25 to 35') ('female', 'age 19 to 24')
>>>
```

Numbers

While numbers are fundamental to programming, they can sometimes feel complicated.

Python, however, makes it really easy to work with them. Assigning a number to a variable is pretty straightforward and follows exactly the same process as other data types.

Python allows you to create a variable that holds a whole number (integer) or a decimal number (floating-point/float).

What this does is allow you to perform a whole variety of mathematical operations and calculations using Python. In the same way, words are stored in string variables, numbers can be stored as numeric variables and used in pretty much the same way as you would with words.

We can experiment with numbers and text in a whole lot of different ways. Open Python and try this,

- age=43

- print('my age is', age)

```
IDLE Shell 3.12.0
File Edit Shell Debug Options Window Help
    Python 3.12.0 (tags/v3.12.0:0fb18b0, Oct  2 2023, 13:03:39) [MSC v.1935 64 bit (
    AMD64)] on win32
    Type "help", "copyright", "credits" or "license()" for more information.
>>> age=43
>>> print('my age is',age)
    my age is 43
>>>
```

Next, let's play with integers using the same text string.

- age=43

- future_age=+7

- print('I will be', age+future_age,'in 7 years time')

```
Python 3.12.0 (tags/v3.12.0:0fb18b0, Oct  2 2023, 13:03:39) [MSC v.1935 64 bit (
AMD64)] on win32
Type "help", "copyright", "credits" or "license()" for more information.
>>> age=43
>>> future_age=+7
>>> print('I will be', age+future_age,'in 7 years time')
I will be 50 in 7 years time
>>>
```

Let's try one more with floats or floating points. We're going to convert Celsius to Fahrenheit now, using Python.

Enter the following,

- temperature_celsius = 25.5

- temperature_fahrenheit = (temperature_celsius * 9/5) + 32

- print('The temperature in Celsius is', temperature_celsius, 'degrees.')

- The temperature in Celsius is 25.5 degrees.

- print('The temperature in Fahrenheit is approximately', temperature_fahrenheit, 'degrees.')

```
Python 3.12.0 (tags/v3.12.0:0fb18b0, Oct  2 2023, 13:03:39) [MSC v.1935 64 bit (AMD64)] on win32
Type "help", "copyright", "credits" or "license()" for more information.
>>> temperature_celsius = 25.5
>>> temperature_fahrenheit = (temperature_celsius * 9/5) + 32
>>> print('The temperature in Celsius is', temperature_celsius, 'degrees.')
The temperature in Celsius is 25.5 degrees.
>>> print('The temperature in Fahrenheit is approximately', temperature_fahrenheit, 'degrees.')
The temperature in Fahrenheit is approximately 77.9 degrees.
>>>
```

A Word on Operators

I know we're skipping back nearly an entire chapter, but since you've now graduated to more complex data inputs, there's something I'd like to draw your attention to.

Variables that hold integers or floats can be manipulated by using the most basic arithmetic operators. For instance, you can subtract, add, multiply, and divide. Whenever you work with these operators you will create an expression instead of a statement—a code that has to be processed by the computer system in order to find the value.

Take a look at the code below.

tshirts=6+6

jeans=8-2

socks=7*2

clothing=tshirts+jeans+socks

clothing

```
Python 3.12.0 (tags/v3.12.0:0fb18b0, Oct  2 2023, 13:03:39) [MSC v.1935 64 bit (
AMD64)] on win32
Type "help", "copyright", "credits" or "license()" for more information.
>>> tshirts=6+6
>>> jeans=8-2
>>> socks=7*2
>>> clothing=tshirts+jeans+socks
>>> clothing
32
>>>
```

Now, if you did the calculation in your head and your answer is 50, this isn't Python's fault. If you think back to elementary math, PEMDAS (BODMAS for those outside of the USA) needs to be applied and Python knows that.

Go ahead and apply PEMDAS or BODMAS—whichever you use—and you'll see that Python is correct. This is because the program is capable of evaluating the expression, and then deciding which blocks need to be processed before others. In other words, it follows an operator precedence.

The example above uses integers, but if you were to use floating points, the same rules would apply. In addition, Python will convert an integer to a floating point or even a string. Any number can be converted to an integer by typing *int (n)*, or a float by typing *float (n)*, or a string by typing str (objectname). These functions follow the same structure as the print function and once you've declared the function you want to use, all you'll need to do is place the value, variable, or object between parenthesis so that you can manipulate it.

Give it a try by opening Python and entering,

- float(10)

- int(10.4)

Now that you know the basics, let's get to an exercise so that you can test your knowledge of this chapter.

Foundational Exercise for Labels and Variables

In this exercise, you're going to create a program that acts as a simple calculator. The end user will need to be able to perform basic mathematical operations. Your program will need to,

1. Write a welcome message.

2. Enter two numbers.

3. Choose an operation using the labels for these operations.

4. Calculate the result.

5. Display the result.

Play around with different strings of numbers, welcome messages, and operations to see if you really have the hang of things. My solution is on the next page.

```
Python 3.12.0 (tags/v3.12.0:0fb18b0, Oct  2 2023, 13:03:39) [MSC v.1935 64 bit (AMD64)] on win32
Type "help", "copyright", "credits" or "license()" for more information.
>>> print('Welcome to your calculator')
Welcome to your calculator
>>> num1=20.5
>>> num2=7.2
>>> print(num1+num2)
27.7
>>> print(num1-num2)
13.3
>>> print(num1*num2)
147.6
>>> print(num1/num2)
2.8472222222222223
>>> print(num1%num2)
6.1
>>> 
```

CHAPTER 5

Breaking Down Lists, Tuples, Sets, and Dictionaries

When it comes to programming, data comes in different forms, and learning to manage your data with speed and efficiency is a fundamental skill. Python provides its users with four powerful data structures, these being

- Lists—ordered collections of items that are capable of holding elements of different data types.

- Tuples—similar to lists, but immutable (elements cannot be changed after creation.)

- Sets—collections of unique elements.

- Dictionaries—key-value pairs where values can be accessed by their associated keys.

By the end of this chapter, you'll have a good idea of these essential data structures. This will allow you to unlock each of these structure's full potential and solve real-world problems by building Python programs.

Lists

A list is an ordered collection of elements and can contain a mix of different data types. Their elements are indexed which allows you to access and manipulate them easily. These lists are used for various programming tasks including data management and building dynamic structures.

You can create a list by enclosing elements in square brackets, for example,

- clothing=['tshirts','jeans','socks','jackets']

You can store as many items or values as you like within a list and recall each one seamlessly. The above example uses string values. This means you will need to use parentheses to let Python know that these are string values.

Let's say you have created a list and have forgotten what's on it. You don't even remember how many items were on the list in the first place. You'd need to ascertain,

- How many components are on your list
- The value of the individual components

All you would need is the len() function which would display the length of the characters, components, or items within a variable or list—we'll go into further detail on the len function a little later.

For now, let's practice with lists.

Exercise

In this exercise, you're going to;

- Create a list of numbers. [2, 4, 6, 8, 10].
- Next, you're going to write a program to compute and print the sum of the numbers in your list.
- Finally, you need to verify that the program works correctly by testing it with different lists.

Give it a go and then check out the solution below.

```
IDLE Shell 3.12.0
File Edit Shell Debug Options Window Help
    Python 3.12.0 (tags/v3.12.0:0fb18b0, Oct  2 2023, 13:03:39) [MSC v.1935 64 bit (
    AMD64)] on win32
    Type "help", "copyright", "credits" or "license()" for more information.
>>> numbers=[2, 4, 6, 8, 10]
>>> sum_of_numbers=sum(numbers)
>>> print('The sum of the numbers is:', sum_of_numbers)
    The sum of the numbers is: 30
>>>
```

Tuples

If you've been interested in programming before, the word Tuple would have definitely come up. Tuples are a collection of ordered and immutable elements. While lists can be changed once they've been created, tuples cannot be modified at all. Tuples are used to store pieces of information that are both related and that should remain unchanged.

Unknowingly, you've already worked with tuples. Take a look at the elements that are enclosed in brackets, below.

- fruits=('apple','banana','cherry')

Do you recognize the code above?

You can access your tuple elements by their index, just like you did with your lists. Indexing starts from 0 so if you wanted to access apple, you'd need to input 0,

- first_fruit = fruits[0]

Remember, tuples are immutable so you can't change their elements. For you to make changes, you need to create an entirely new tuple. Let's say we created our fruits and forgot to add kiwi to it. If you were to try to add kiwi to this tuple now, it would result in an error.

```
*IDLE Shell 3.12.0*
File Edit Shell Debug Options Window Help
    Python 3.12.0 (tags/v3.12.0:0fb18b0, Oct  2 2023, 13:03:39) [MSC v.1935 64 bit (
    AMD64)] on win32
    Type "help", "copyright", "credits" or "license()" for more information.
>>> fruits = ('apple', 'banana', 'cherry')
>>> first_fruit=fruits[0]
>>> fruits[1]='kiwi'
    Traceback (most recent call last):
      File "<pyshell#2>", line 1, in <module>
        fruits[1]='kiwi'
    TypeError: 'tuple' object does not support item assignment
>>>
```

A nice function that Python has is the ability to pack multiple values into a tuple and then unpack them into variables.

Okay, let's have a look at a real-world exercise using tuples.

Exercise

1. Define a tuple for coordinates 3 and 4.

2. Access and print these coordinates under x and y.

Give it a go and then look at the solution on the following page.

```
Python 3.12.0 (tags/v3.12.0:0fb18b0, Oct  2 2023, 13:03:39) [MSC v.1935 64 bit (AMD64)] on win32
Type "help", "copyright", "credits" or "license()" for more information.
>>> coordinates=(3,4)
>>> x,y=coordinates
>>> print('x:',x)
x: 3
>>> print('y',y)
y 4
>>> 
```

Sets

A set is a collection of unordered, unique elements in Python. You would use sets when you need to store multiple items that are not indexed and where no duplicates are present. Mathematical operations like union, difference, and intersection use sets to good use.

To create sets, you would enclose your desired elements in curly brackets {} or by using the set() constructor.

Using the fruits example above, sets would be created as follows,

- fruits={'apple', 'banana', 'cherry'}

For you to access it you would need to use *in*. The reason for this is that sets are unordered and because of this, you can't access set elements by index. Let's give it a try.

- if "apple" in fruits:
  - print("Yes, 'apple' is in the set.")

You can add and remove elements when using sets. For example,

- fruits.add("orange") would add orange to your set
- fruits.remove("apple" would remove apple from the set.

Remember we mentioned that sets support set operations? These include union, intersection, and difference.

In our section exercise below, we're going to put your knowledge of sets to the test, so let's get to it.

Exercise

1. Create two sets, set1, and set2, with some common and unique elements. You can use 1, 2, 3, 4, 5, and 3, 4, 5, 6, 7.

2. Next, print the elements in each set.

3. Now, calculate and print the union of set1 and set2.

4. Calculate and print the intersection of set1 and set2.

5. Calculate and print the set difference (elements in set1 but not in set2).

6. Calculate and print the set difference (elements in set2 but not in set1).

Give it a try and when you're ready, take a look at the solution.

```
Python 3.12.0 (tags/v3.12.0:0fb18b0, Oct  2 2023, 13:03:39) [MSC v.1935 64 bit (AMD64)] on win32
Type "help", "copyright", "credits" or "license()" for more information.
>>> set1 = {1, 2, 3, 4, 5}
>>> set2 = {3, 4, 5, 6, 7}
>>> print("Set 1:", set1)
Set 1: {1, 2, 3, 4, 5}
>>> print("Set 2:", set2)
Set 2: {3, 4, 5, 6, 7}
>>> union_set = set1.union(set2)
>>> print("Union of Set 1 and Set 2:", union_set)
Union of Set 1 and Set 2: {1, 2, 3, 4, 5, 6, 7}
>>> intersection_set = set1.intersection(set2)
>>> print("Intersection of Set 1 and Set 2:", intersection_set)
Intersection of Set 1 and Set 2: {3, 4, 5}
>>> difference_set2 = set2.difference(set1)
>>> print("Set Difference (Set 2 - Set 1):", difference_set2)
Set Difference (Set 2 - Set 1): {6, 7}
>>>
```

Dictionaries

Finally, we're going to take a look at dictionaries. This versatile data structure is used to store key-value pairs. Sometimes called an associative array or hash map (not in Python though), dictionaries are defined by curly brackets{} and contain keys and their associated values.

You would therefore create a dictionary by providing a set of key-value pairs that are contained within your curly brackets. Here's an example,

- my_dict = {"name": "John", "age": 30, "city": "New York"}

Go ahead and input this into Python, as we will be using this dictionary to build on throughout this section.

You can now access values in a dictionary by referencing the relevant keys.

- name=my_dict["name"]

Because dictionaries are mutable, you can change their values and add new key-value pairs to your dictionary as well as remove existing ones.

Here's an example of changing the values,

- my_dict["age"]=31

This will update the value associated with the key "age" and by entering

- my_dict["country"]="USA"

you add a new key-value pair, while

- del my_dict["city"]

removes the key "city" as well as its associated value.

Finally, you loop through dictionaries by using the *for* loop.

- for key,value in my_dict.items():

- print(key,value)

Exercise

For this exercise, you're going to create a dictionary to store contact information. Your example should contain space for a name, email address, and telephone number.

Then, you're going to print the name, email, address, and telephone number. Remember, when using dictionaries you need to use the dictionary *and* corresponding key to access the value.

Give it a go and then look at the solution.

> ***Pro Tip:** When creating this dictionary you should open your curly brackets before you add your data and close the curly brackets after.*

```
IDLE Shell 3.12.0                                          —    □    ×
File Edit Shell Debug Options Window Help
    Python 3.12.0 (tags/v3.12.0:0fb18b0, Oct  2 2023, 13:03:39) [MSC v.1935 64 bit (
    AMD64)] on win32
    Type "help", "copyright", "credits" or "license()" for more information.
>>> contact={
...     'name':'John Doe',
...     'email':'john@example.com',
...     'phone':'+123456789'
...     }
>>> print(contact['name'])
    John Doe
>>> print(contact['email'])
    john@example.com
>>> print(contact['phone'])
    +123456789
>>>
```

Foundational Exercise for Lists, Tuples, Sets, and Dictionaries

Right! You've reached the end of this chapter and are well on your way to creating your first programming with Python. Let's test your knowledge of this chapter before moving on to intermediate programming knowledge.

In this exercise, you're going to create a Python program that incorporates all of the elements you've learned in Chapter 5.

You'll need to

1. Create a list of numbers (integers or floats).

2. Create a tuple with a few items (strings or numbers).

3. Create a set with unique items (names or cities).

4. Create a dictionary with key-value pairs (names as keys and ages as values).

Once you have done this, you're going to put your knowledge into action by

1. Adding a number number to your list.

2. Changing one item in your tuple.

3. Adding a new item to your set.

4. Adding a new key-value pair to your dictionary.

Finally, once you have completed all these steps, you'll need to display your modified list, tuple set, and dictionary.

```
Python 3.12.0 (tags/v3.12.0:0fb18b0, Oct  2 2023, 13:03:39) [MSC v.1935 64 bit (
AMD64)] on win32
Type "help", "copyright", "credits" or "license()" for more information.
>>> numbers_list=[1,2,3,4,5]
>>> items_tuple=("apple","banana","cherry")
>>> unique_set={"New York","Los Angeles","Chicago"}
>>> ages_dict={"Alice":30,"Bob":25,"Charlie":35}
>>> numbers_list.append(6)
>>> items_list=list(items_tuple)
>>> items_list[1]="kiwi"
>>> items_tuple=tuple(items_list)
>>> unique_set.add("Miami")
>>> ages_dict["David"]=28
>>> print("Modified List:",numbers_list)
Modified List: [1, 2, 3, 4, 5, 6]
>>> print("Modified Tuple:",items_tuple)
Modified Tuple: ('apple', 'kiwi', 'cherry')
>>> print("Modified Set:",unique_set)
Modified Set: {'Miami', 'New York', 'Chicago', 'Los Angeles'}
>>> print("Modified Dictionary:",ages_dict)
Modified Dictionary: {'Alice': 30, 'Bob': 25, 'Charlie': 35, 'David': 28}
>>>
```

How did you do?

CHAPTER 6

Functions, Modules, and Files in Python

Before we begin with this chapter, I'd like to congratulate you on graduating to intermediate Python programming. You've stuck around, dealt with the errors, and experimented your way to success; Well done!

In this chapter, you're going to learn about functions, modules, and files when using Python. These critical elements will help you in a number of ways when it comes to programming.

Firstly, functions, modules, and files allow you to break down your code into smaller, reusable components that ensure your code is organized and manageable. You will be able to write functions for specific tasks and then call those functions whenever you need a task performed.

Added to this, learning about files specifically, enables you to work with external data sources so that you can read, write, and manipulate data in a whole lot of different formats. This is, of course, essential for processing and analyzing data in real-world applications.

Most importantly, functions, modules, and file handling elevate your proficiency in functions and are pretty fundamental skills when developing software. These three Python functions will ensure you're prepared for work in the real world where you will need to collaborate with other developers on Python-based projects. So, let's get into it!

Functions

A function is a block of named code that performs a specific set of tasks or a singular task.

Coding requires smaller, manageable chunks you can work with and functions provide you with the modularized code. Using functions comes with a number of benefits that include

- readability—your code is far more readable and organized into logical components.

- modularity—code is divided into reusable blocks so that you can write a function or task and call it whenever you need to.

- reusability—once a function is defined it can be called on multiple times within your code and saves you from having to duplicate work.

- testing—functions allow you to test your code and debug only specific parts so that you can isolate and troubleshoot function issues efficiently.

Functions are created using the *def* keyword which is then followed by the function name and a pair of parenthesis. For example,

- def greet(name):

- print("Hello, " + name + "!")

Here, *greet* is the function name while (name) is the parameter the function will take.

To use this function you would need to call it by its name so that you pass the required arguments within the parentheses. If we expand upon the example above, this would be,

- greet("Jane")

This is a call to the greet function with the argument now being "Jane" and the goal would be to bring "Hello, Jane!" to the console. But enough of this theoretical stuff, let's open Python and try a real-world example using Python's built-in function for common math operations.

Modules

Modules are files that contain Python code. This code within a module can define anything from functions to classes and variables and can even execute code. Modules provide you with a way to organize and structure your Python code into separate files. This makes your code more manageable.

In other words, modules allow you to organize the elements and components inside your code, providing you with an auto contained package of variables. Modules also allow you to reuse code, using data services, and linking individual files so that you can broaden your program.

For programs that are more complex (and what you are going to be doing from here on out in this book), modules assist in being able to add old, simple codes to more complex applications and tasks.

Modules also allow you a way to divide your code into smaller chunks so that you have smaller "puzzle" pieces that can be added to create a bigger, more cohesive picture. Creating modules is fairly simple and can be done by saving a file with the *.py* extension. Your file will be stored in the folder of your preference that can later be imported.

Creating Your Own Modules

Let's create your own module now, by saving your Python code in a *.py* file. For the purposes of this section, you'll also be taught how to import your module to your program.

Go ahead and open Python, and let's begin creating an interactable program

- print("Welcome to Python, User")

```
IDLE Shell 3.12.0                                                    —    □   ×
File Edit Shell Debug Options Window Help
    Python 3.12.0 (tags/v3.12.0:0fb18b0, Oct  2 2023, 13:03:39) [MSC v.1935 64 bit (
    AMD64)] on win32
    Type "help", "copyright", "credits" or "license()" for more information.
>>> print("Welcome to Python, User")
    Welcome to Python, User
>>> |




                                                                        Ln: 5  Col: 0
```

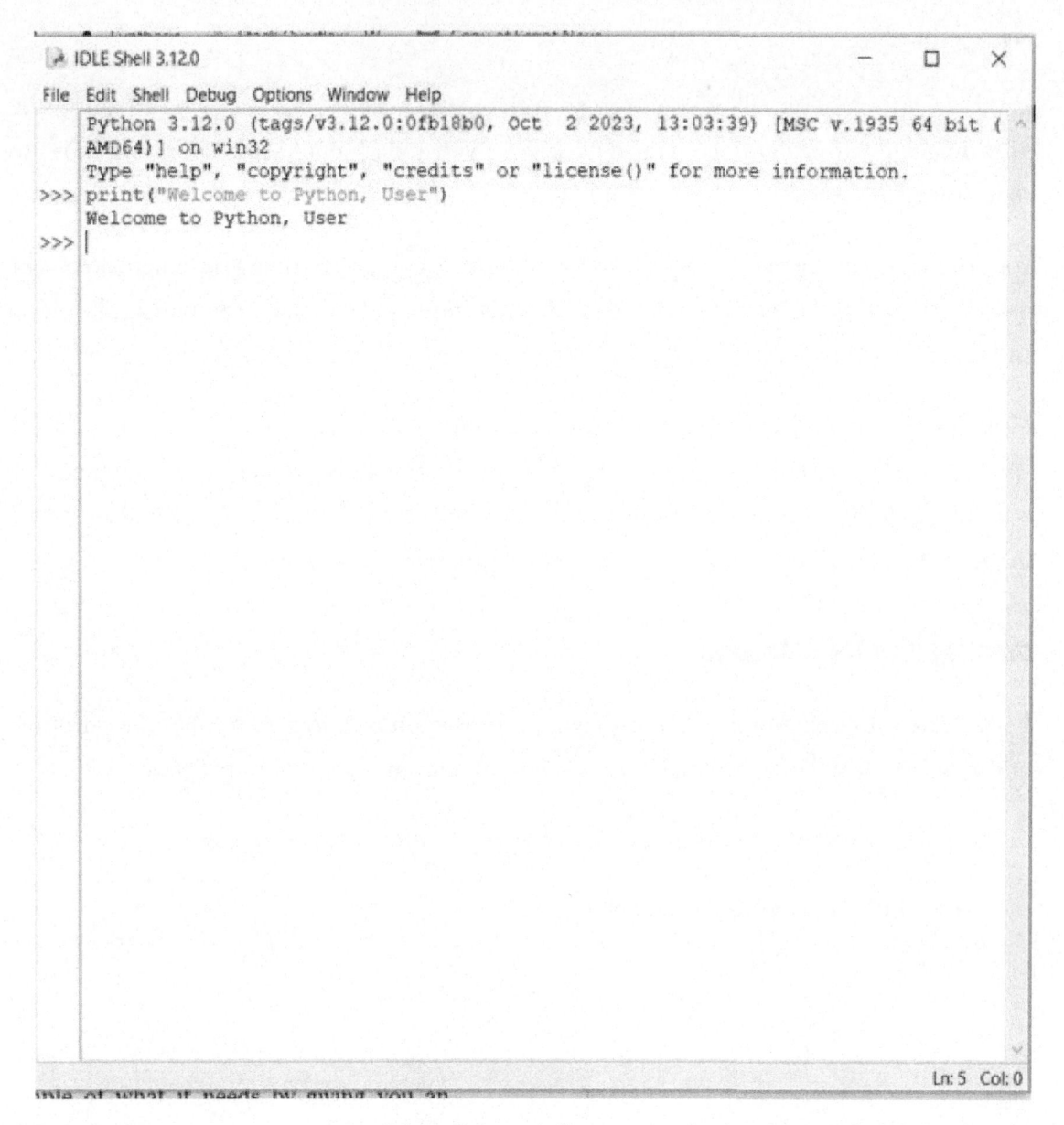

Next you're going to navigate to *File* in the top left corner and select *New File*. This will open a new Untitled document. Do not close IDLE.

This Untitled document is where you're going to enter your workable code. Once your document is open, enter the following.

- name=input("enter your name: ")

- print("Your name is "+name)

Before running your code, you're going to need to save your file. This can be done by navigating to *File* once more and selecting *Save As*. Make sure you're naming your file with an appropriate name. Let's go ahead and name this one Read-Print-User.

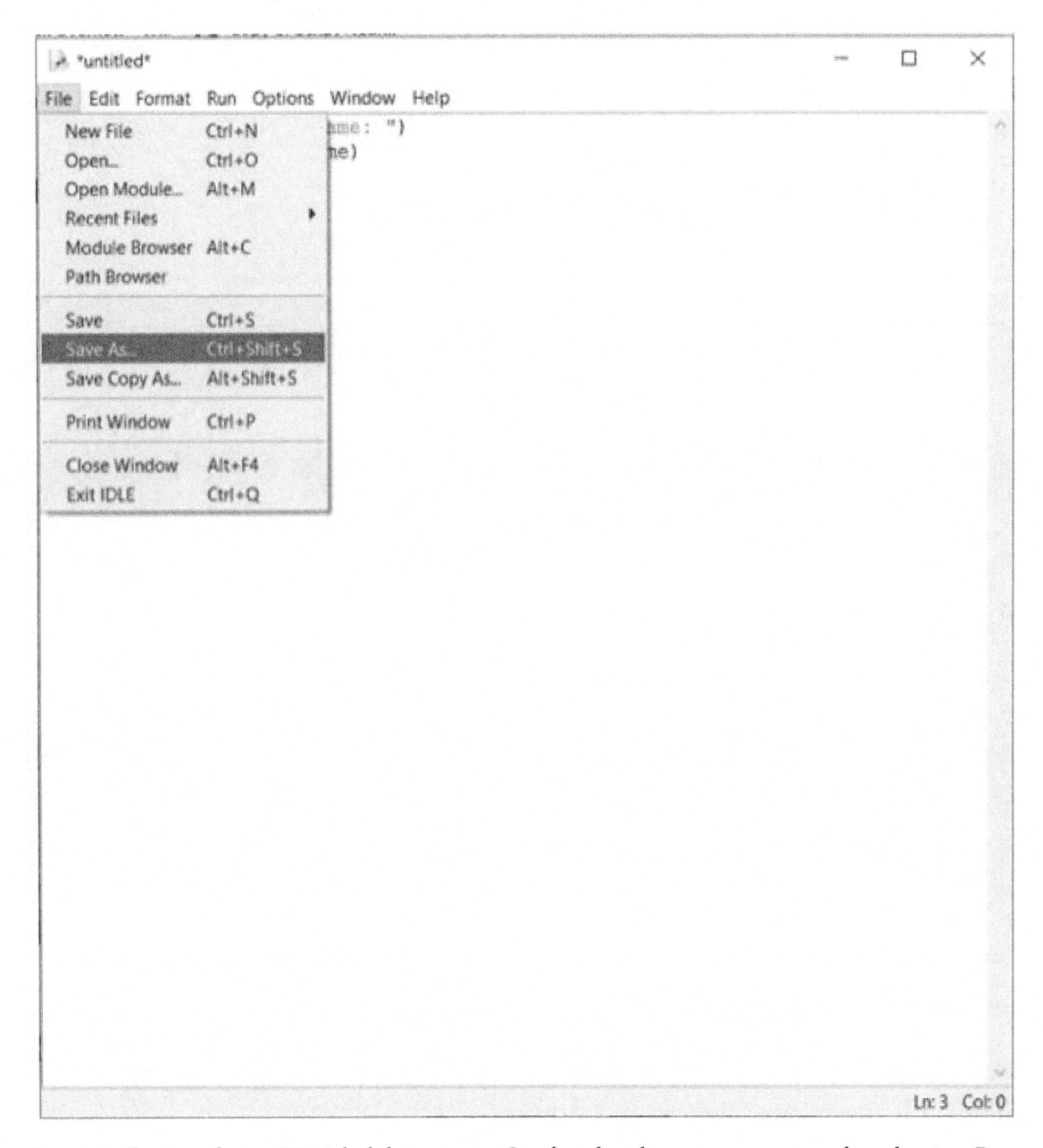

Once you've saved your Untitled document, Go ahead and run your program by selecting *Run Module* or by pressing F5.

IDLE will now restart and your interactive program will be ready to use. Try it out.

```
IDLE Shell 3.12.0                                              —    ☐   ×
File Edit Shell Debug Options Window Help
    Python 3.12.0 (tags/v3.12.0:0fb18b0, Oct  2 2023, 13:03:39) [MSC v.1935 64 bit (
    AMD64)] on win32
    Type "help", "copyright", "credits" or "license()" for more information.
>>> print("Welcome to Python, User")
    Welcome to Python, User
>>>
    = RESTART: C:/Users/      /AppData/Local/Programs/Python/Python312/Read-Print-Use
    r.py
    enter your name: Jane
    Your name is Jane
>>>
```

We can now modify and expand upon your program by going back to your saved file. You're now going to add first name and last name to your program.

Before the field name, you're now going to add an f for first name and enter your message appropriately with ("Your first name is "+name).

Next, you'll need to add a new variable for last name. This can be done by pressing Enter to create a new line spacer to input an lname for last name and enter your appropriate message as

- lname=input("enter your last name: ")

Finally, you need to correct your print string.

- print("Your name is "+fname +lname)

Save your updated code before running the module.

```
fname=input("enter your first name: ")
lname=input("enter your last name: ")
print("Your name is " +fname + lname)
```

Running your program will now open a new IDLE window and you'll be able to enter your first name, last name, and your program will run by responding "Your name is..."

```
enter your first name: Jane
enter your last name: Doe
Your name is JaneDoe
>>>
```

Congratulations! You've just completed your first interactable program using modules. As you can see, it's really easy to go in, create your code, and make changes when using this Python feature.

Importing Python Modules

Modules can contain definitions of a function and even statements. If your code is correct, these are executable. It is possible to initialize a module but only execute when your module is on the import statement.

There are a number of steps that need to be followed when importing a Python module. Either, you can search for the module through the module search path, compile to bytecode, or finally, execute the byte-code of your module, building an object that defines it. Searching for a module is fairly simple in new versions of Python. All you need to do is navigate to *File, Open Module*. This will bring up a list of saved modules on your PC that can be opened/imported.

Namespace in Modules

Modules are files and Python creates a module object where all the names that you assigned in your first module-file will be contained. Now, I know that sounds like a mouthful, all it means is that namespaces are places where all the names that are going to become attributes are created.

Attributes on the other hand are the names that have been assigned to a value. These are considered of a higher level on a module file and that do not belong to a function or a class.

A function that has been defined will only set the parameters and then give it a name. In other words, you have to set the structure for the block of codes if you're going to execute it by creating another function.

Files In Python

A collection of data that is stored on a storage device, like your hard drive or your memory is a file. Files are stored in different types of data. These include text, binary, images, and so much more.

In Python, there are built-in functions and methods so that you can work with files, and this allows you to read from and write to these files seamlessly. To open a file you first need to open it.

This can be done by navigating to the *File, Open* function, or by using the open() common and specifying the file path and the mode. For example,

- file = open('example.txt', 'r')

Here is a list of file modes.

1. 'r': Read mode (default). Opens the file for reading.

2. 'w': Write mode. Opens the file for writing. Creates a new file or truncates an existing file.

3. 'a': Append mode. Opens the file for writing. Creates a new file or appends to an existing file.

4. 'b': Binary mode. Opens the file in binary mode (e.g., 'rb' or 'wb').

Best Practices for Handling Files

Always make sure to close files after you have used them. You can use the *with* statement for automatic closing (context manager, and check that the file actually exists before you open it.

Functions, Modules, and Files Exercise

This is going to be a fun, interactive exercise that is going to allow you to write a fully functional, interactive program by the end of your programming. Open up Python IDLE and then open a new file.

Let's get to it! I'm not going to tell you what your objective is during this exercise, we're simply going to code together and see where it leads us to! Once you have opened a new file, go ahead and save it as Quiz Game. Ready? Let's get to it!

CHAPTER 7

Object-Oriented Programming Made Easy

Object-oriented programming (OOP) is a programming paradigm. These paradigms include functional, procedural, declarative programming, and so on. OOP organizes code based on objects. These objects represent real-world units or entities and condense the functions that operate on the data.

Here are some of the key concepts of OOP.

1. Classes and Objects

- Classes are a blueprint or template that is used for creating objects. It defines the attributes (properties) as well as the methods (behaviors) that the objects of the class will have.

- Objects are an instance of a class—the solid entity created based on the definition of a class.

1. Encapsulation

- Encapsulation includes attributes (the bundling of your data) and functions (methods). These operate on the data you've captured within a single unit.

- Encapsulation also restricts access to some of the object's components for data hiding.

1. Inheritance

- This is a mechanism in which a new class, subclass, or derived class inherits the properties and behaviors of an existing class—sometimes called a parent or base class.

- It allows for reusability and the creation of a hierarchy of class.

1. Polymorphism

- Polymorphism allows objects to be treated as an instance of the parent class. This can be done even if they are subclasses or instances.

- This allows for flexibility when using different classes through a common interface.

Now that you know some of the key concepts of OOP, we're going to focus on the most used of these key aspects, classes, and objects.

The Relationship Between Classes and Objects

When using OOP, the relationship between objects and classes is absolutely critical. Classes are the blueprint or template used for creating objects. They define the data and methods that the objects of a class will have. Objects, on the other hand, are instances of a class. It's concrete and based on a class definition. These objects must have specific values for their attributes and will perform the actions defined by the class method.

I know this sounds really confusing, so let's look at an example.

- def __init__(self, make, model, year):
  - self.make = make
  - self.model = model
  - self.year = year
  - def start_engine(self):
- print(f"The {self.year} {self.model}'s engine is now running.")

If we take a look at the above code, car is the class defining the blueprint for cars. Car 1 and car

2 are objects of the car class.

```
class Car:
    def __init__(self, make, model, year):
        self.make = make
        self.model = model
        self.year = year

    def start_engine(self):
        print(f"The {self.year} {self.model}'s engine is now running.")
```

Each of these objects now needs its own unique values for the attributes, these being the make, model, and year.

```
File  Edit  Format  Run  Options  Window  Help
class Car:
    def __init__(self, make, model, year):
        self.make = make
        self.model = model
        self.year = year

    def start_engine(self):
        print(f"The {self.year} {self.model}'s engine is now running.")


car1 = Car ("Toyata", "Camry", 2020)
car2 = Car ("Honda", "Accord", 2022)
```

Okay, so a class is a blueprint or template, an object is the instance created from a class, and relationship are objects are instances of classes. Classes define the structure and objects are specific instances of unique data. This means that multiple objects can be created from the same class.

Magic Methods

In Python, structural methods are referred to as "Special methods," or "Magic methods." These are double underscore (dunder) methods and are denoted by a double underscore before and after a name. They are used to define how objects of a class behave with respect to certain operations in our previous exercise, we used the special method __init__(self) but there are other special methods that you can use. These are,

- The constructor method—when an object is created to initialize its attributes denoted by __init__(self).

- String representation of an object when str() is called. This is most often used for the print function and is denoted by __str__(self).

- The string representation of an object usually used by the repr() function can be defined as an official string representation of an object by using __repr__(self).

- To return the length of an object when len() is called, __len(self) can be used.

- Finally, to define the behavior of the + operator when it is applied to objects of a specific class __add__(self, other): is used.

Each of these special/magic methods allows you to customize how your class behaves in terms of different contexts. This makes your classes more versatile. Let's take a look at an example.

Open a new file, saving it as Person-Example.py. Once you've done that, go ahead and enter the following code.

- class Person:

    - def __init__(self, name, age):

        - self.name = name

        - self.age = age

- person1= Person("Jane", 45)

- print(person1.name)

- print(person1.age)

Save and run your program.

```
Python 3.12.0 (tags/v3.12.0:0fb18b0, Oct  2 2023, 13:03:39) [MSC v.1935 64 bit (
AMD64)] on win32
Type "help", "copyright", "credits" or "license()" for more information.
>>>
= RESTART: C:/Users/        /AppData/Local/Programs/Python/Python312/Person-Example
.py
Jane
45
>>>
```

The final thing we need to look at as far as special/magic methods are concerned, is Destructor methods.

This is implemented using the double underscore and del (__del__). The use of __del__ is less commonly used in Python because the program has an automatic garbage collection. Having said that, you can still use __del__ to destroy an object, returning its reference to zero.

Because Python has its own garbage collection, we're not going to create an exercise for Destructor methods but feel free to experiment with this as much as you want.

OOP in Action Exercise

Right, future programmer, it's time to step it up and create more complex programs that use the OOP principles you've learned. While this chapter is quite short, OOP can be difficult to wrap your mind around and chances are you've experienced a fair share of errors while experimenting with the program. Don't worry though, mistakes are only stepping stones to success, so keep trying.

We're going to create a simple program that models a basic banking system. This will use an *Account* object.

As with the previous exercise, you don't need to worry about following instructions. Instead, you're going to code along with me. I am, however, not going to provide the correct spacing for your code. This is going to be entirely up to you.

Begin by opening IDLE and creating a new file. Save this file as Account-Exercise.py. Make sure to save and run your program often to ensure you fix bugs as they occur. And if you want to try and create your own program, go ahead! If not, our next chapter will provide you with a programming challenge that you can move on to once you're confident enough to.

- class Account:

- def __init__(self, account_holder, balance=0):

- self.account_holder = account_holder

- self.balance = balance

- def deposit(self, amount):

- if amount > 0:

- self.balance += amount
- print(f"Deposit ${amount}. New balance: ${self.balance}")
- else:
- print("Invalid deposit amount.")
- def withdraw(self, amount):
- if 0 < amount <= self.balance:
- self.balance -= amount
- print(f"Withdrew ${amount}. New balance: ${self.balance}")
- else:
- print("Invalid withdrawal amount or insufficient funds.")
- def get_balance(self):
- return self.balance
- if __name__ == "__main__":
- account1 = Account("John Doe", 1000)
- account2 = Account("Jane Smith")
- account1.deposit(500)
- account1.withdraw(200)
- print(f"{account1.account_holder}'s final balance: ${account1.get_balance()}")
- print(f"{account2.account_holder}'s final balance: ${account2.get_balance()}")

Code

```
class Account:
    def __init__(self, account_holder, balance=0):
        self.account_holder = account_holder
        self.balance = balance

    def deposit(self, amount):
        if amount > 0:
            self.balance += amount
            print(f"Deposit ${amount}. New balance: ${self.balance}")
        else:
            print("Invalid deposit amount.")

    def withdraw(self, amount):
        if 0 < amount <= self.balance:
            self.balance -= amount
            print(f"Withdrew ${amount}. New balance: ${self.balance}")
        else:
            print("Invalid withdrawal amount or insufficient funds.")

    def get_balance(self):
        return self.balance

if __name__ == "__main__":

    account1 = Account("John Doe", 1000)
    account2 = Account("Jane Smith")

    account1.deposit(500)
    account1.withdraw(200)

    print(f"{account1.account_holder}'s final balance: ${account1.get_balance()}")
    print(f"{account2.account_holder}'s final balance: ${account2.get_balance()}")
```

Solution: Program

```
Python 3.12.0 (tags/v3.12.0:0fb18b0, Oct  2 2023, 13:03:39) [MSC v.1935 64 bit (AMD64)] on win32
Type "help", "copyright", "credits" or "license()" for more information.
>>>
= RESTART: C:/Users/    /AppData/Local/Programs/Python/Python312/Account Example.py
Deposit $500. New balance: $1500
Withdrew $200. New balance: $1300
John Doe's final balance: $1300
Jane Smith's final balance: $0
>>>
```

Take Advantage of Your Cheat Sheet

Sometimes you just don't have the time to scan through an entire book to try and remember something you have learned. Even the most seasoned programmers have errors and lapses in memory and if you've forgotten something right in the middle of coding your next epic program!

I know exactly how frustrating this can be and I've found a solution—*The Ultimate Python Cheat Sheet*. This easy cheat sheet provides you with a space that documents common Python types, descriptions, and syntaxes so that you don't have to search through pages of information!

Simply scan the QR Code below to unlock your free gift.

CHAPTER 8

Your First Interactive Program Using Multiline Statements

Welcome to your first interactive program using multiline statements. Now I hear you say, "Narry! We've been programming all along!" and you wouldn't be wrong. What makes this exercise different is that you're going to be given instructions on what your program should do along with some basic hints and guides, and the rest will be up to you.

For this task, you're going to create, run, and experiment with an interactive task manager program. This will help you to put all of your knowledge into practice while putting the fundamental concepts of Python that you have learned to the test.

So what's the end goal?

This program is going to be created to provide users with an interactive menu where they can select the actions they want to perform. While programming your task manager, you will need to follow the prompts below and run your program so that you can test whether or not a user can interact with the program. Added to this, you're going to take on lists of tasks, creating multiline statements that add up to a fully functional program.

So what should your program do?

You're going to create a task manager where your end users can

- Add tasks to the task list—users should be prompted to enter the name of the task they want to add.

- Mark tasks as complete—users should be asked to enter the index of the task they have marked as complete.

- View tasks that still require completion along with any completion status.

- Finally, your program will need to allow users to exit the program.

Prompts and Hints

1. Open your preferred text editor or IDLE new file—I prefer to save this file right from the outset to prevent my work from getting lost, but it's up to you.

2. Begin to write your code. Save often and if you get stuck, try to troubleshoot the issue yourself—if you can't solve the issue, have a look at my solution below.

3. Run your program often to make sure that you can debug small chunks of codes—save and use F5 to run.

4. Test your program by interacting with it—a good program should be user-friendly and the only way to know if your program is great for the people using it is to test it yourself.

5. Make sure that your user can exit the program.

6. Customize and experiment with your program—while I will provide you with the "bones" of a functional program, it's up to you to finetune and create something amazing.

And now you have all of your instructions and hints you need. Enjoy your coding experience and when you're ready, check my "bare bones" program below.

Basic Program Example

```python
class TaskManager:
    def __init__(self):
        self.tasks = []
    def add_task(self, task):
        self.tasks.append({"task": task, "completed": False})
        print(f"Task '{task}' added.")
    def mark_completed(self, task_index):
        if 0 <= task_index < len(self.tasks):
            self.tasks[task_index]["completed"] = True
            print(f"Task '{self.tasks[task_index]['task']}' marked as completed.")
        else:
            print("Invalid task index.")
    def view_tasks(self):
        if self.tasks:
            print("Current Task List:")
            for index, task_info in enumerate(self.tasks):
                status = "Completed" if task_info["completed"] else "Pending"
                print(f"{index + 1}. {task_info['task']} - {status}")
        else:
            print("Task list is empty.")
#Building of Interactive Program
if __name__ == "__main__":
    task_manager = TaskManager()
while True:
    print("\nOptions:")
```

```
Python 3.12.0 (tags/v3.12.0:0fb18b0, Oct  2 2023, 13:03:39) [MSC v.1935 64 bit (
AMD64)] on win32
Type "help", "copyright", "credits" or "license()" for more information.
>>>
= RESTART: C:\Users\     \AppData\Local\Programs\Python\Python312\Task-Manager E
xample.py

Options:
1. Add Task
2. Mark Task as Completed
3. View Tasks
4. Exit
Enter your choice (1-4): 1
Enter the task: Write Python Book
Task 'Write Python Book' added.

Options:
1. Add Task
2. Mark Task as Completed
3. View Tasks
4. Exit
Enter your choice (1-4): 3
Current Task List:
1. Write Python Book - Pending

Options:
1. Add Task
2. Mark Task as Completed
3. View Tasks
4. Exit
Enter your choice (1-4):
```

CHAPTER 9

Python for Data Analysis

Data analysis is the use of data analytics tools and different methods to achieve a specific objective or goal. Through close scrutiny, data analysis allows for the transformation and sorting of unprocessed data so that useful, usable information can be obtained.

During the data analytics process, data is collected and inspected for the purposes of investigation, purification, and the removal of NaN values as well as other outliers in the data. This transforms the data being used into a useful product. While there are a number of programs that can be used to perform data analysis, like SAS and Excel, we will be focusing on Python's role in data analysis.

The two basic principles of analyzing data are interpolation and extrapolation. Let's take a look at these two principles in a little bit more detail.

Interpolation is used to estimate the values that fall between the known, measured, and observed data points. It's very useful in filling in any gaps or missing values in a dataset and allows for the estimation of missing values based on the information gained. In a data analysis context, interpolation helps to smooth out data curves and creates a continuous representation of discrete data by filling in any missing values.

Extrapolation is used to predict the estimating values beyond the range of known data. It extends the trend or pattern being observed in the current and existing data to make predictions for values outside of what is currently being observed. Extrapolation assumes that the established trend will continue.

Why Use Python For Data Analysis

When it comes to programming languages, Python has become a go-to, the world over. There are a couple of reasons for this, but it's Python's versatility that attracts most users. Its clear, readable syntax makes it accessible to most users. Aside from this, its rich ecosystem of libraries and frameworks that are specifically designed for data analysis provides tools to users who may otherwise not be able to use the complex systems of other programs. These include Pandas, NumPy, Matplotlib, Seaborn, and Scikit-learn—we'll discuss some of these in later chapters.

Python truly is a program that encourages easy learning, and the community that uses the program is diverse and extremely active. This, of course, allows for much easier troubleshooting and community support. This support is further solidified by the fact that Python is an open-source language. This means users can use it freely, modify, and distribute the software. This open nature allows for collaborative innovation, especially in the realm of data analysis.

Because data processing is a crucial step in the data analysis pipeline, Python is often the preferred program. The cleaning, organizing, and transforming of raw data allows for it to be formatted in a way that is suitable for analysis. Data analysis is a fundamental part of the data preparation processes because it enhances the quality of the data. This makes it far more understandable as well as applicable for analysis.

Data Preprocessing

Data preprocessing includes a number of several steps that are designed to clean, organize, and transform raw data into suitable formats for analysis. These steps may be different depending on what kind of data is being processed and the analysis goal. There are a number of reasons that data preprocessing is required and these include

- improved accuracy—well-organized and clean data facilitates more accurate analysis, eliminating errors and inconsistencies.

- enhanced model performance—ensures high-quality data is produced because preprocessed data contributes to better machine learning models.

- increased analysis efficiency—streamlined data allows for more precise, efficient analysis processing and provides more manageable and focused datasets.

- better interpretability—data that is preprocessed well is far easier to interpret and understand. This allows for analysts and scientists to easily derive meaningful insights and make informed decisions based on the data presented.

- compatibility with algorithms—machine learning algorithms and statistical methods have assumptions about the data they operate on. Data that is preprocessed allows this data to conform to these assumptions and creates a better algorithmic performance.

- provides exploration and visualization—data that has been cleaned and is well-organized is more conducive to in-depth exploration as well as visualization. This enables analysts to identify specific patterns, correlations, and trends more easily and effectively.

- addresses data quality issues—when data is preprocessed it helps to address common data quality issues. These can include missing values, inconsistencies, and outliers that could otherwise compromise the integrity of the data analysis.

Preprocessing Data Step-By-Step

Data preprocessing requires a number of key steps that will organize, clean, and transform raw data into a suitable format for analysis. Now, not all of these steps may apply and the nature of the data, as well as the analysis goals, will determine which of these steps will be taken.

Let's take a look at a general guideline of what these steps might be.

1. Data collection occurs and raw data, from various sources, like databases, APIs, and files is gathered.

2. Data cleaning in which missing data is handled, missing values are removed or replaced, duplicates are removed, and errors corrected occur.

3. Data exploration of the dataset happens so that a deeper understanding of the characteristics is gained and identification of potential issues occurs.

4. Data transformation where the encoding of categorical variables into numeric formats occurs, normalizing of numerical features, and derived features are created. Added to this, outliers are handled.

5. Data reduction where irrelevant features are removed and data is aggregated and summarized.

6. Handling of imbalanced data where imbalances are distributed into classes or categories.

7. Feature engineering where new features are created based on existing ones with the goal to enhance the predictive power of models.

8. Data integration, combining data from multiple sources (if applicable).

9. Data scaling numerical features to ensure uniformity and avoid biases in algorithms that may be sensitive to scale.

10. Dataset split into training and testing sets for evaluation of the model.

11. Document processing which includes the rationale for specific decisions with the aim of reproducibility and collaboration.

12. Iteration so that additional preprocessing steps can be taken if need be.

13. Quality assurance and checks on the processed data to ensure the utmost integrity.

Always keep in mind that these steps can change based on the characteristics of the data as well as the objective of the data analysis. When addressing the unique challenges that come with each dataset, it's important to note that flexibility and adaptability (agile) practices are best.

Handling Missing Data

Handling missing data is an important step in data preprocessing. Python provides its users with a number of libraries that offer tools for managing missing data. The two most common of these are NumPy and Panda.

Using NumPy

NumPy provides users with functions that create arrays with missing values and perform operations that handle missing data.

To identify missing values, you'd need to use *np.isnan(array)*. This identifies missing values in the NumPy array.

To replace missing values, you use *np.nan_to_num(array)*. This replaces Nan values with zeros.

Alternatively you'd use, *np.nanmean(array)* or *np.nanmedian(array)* to replace NaN values with mean or median respectively.

Using Pandas

Pandas that are built on top on NumPy provide a Dataframe structure with powerful tools that can be used to handle missing data.

These include

- identifying missing values

- Use df.isnull() or df.isna() to identify missing values in a DataFrame.

- removing missing values

- Use df.dropna() to remove rows containing any missing values.

- Use df.dropna(axis=1) to remove columns containing any missing values.

- imputing missing values

- Use df.fillna(value) to fill missing values with a specific constant.

- Use df.fillna(df.mean()) or df.fillna(df.median()) to fill missing values with the mean or median.

- interpolation

- Use df.interpolate() to perform linear interpolation for missing values.

- imputing with machine learning models

- Train machine learning models to predict missing values based on other features.

A Word on Scikit-Learn

Scikit-Learn provides users with an Imputer class that handles missing values in a dataset. For beginners, Scikit-Learn offers a powerful and flexible platform for machine learning development and solutions when using Python.

It comes with a consistent and straightforward application programming interface (API) for various machine learning tasks and the uniformity of the interface truly simplifies the process of switching between the different algorithms and models used. It's easy to use meaning beginners and scientists alike can take advantage of the extensive documentation. Added to this, Scikit-Learn includes a comprehensive set of machine learning algorithms that can be used for regression, clustering, classification, and dimensionality reduction.

All of this occurs with efficient implementation because Scikit-Learn is built on top of other numerical and scientific libraries like NumPy and SciPy. This also means it is great for large datasets and complex models.

Impuring with mean and median requires the following code

```
from sklearn.impute import SimpleImputer
imputer = SimpleImputer(strategy='mean')  # or 'median'
df_imputed = pd.DataFrame(imputer.fit_transform(df), columns=df.columns)
```

And, imputing with constant requires

```
imputer = SimpleImputer(strategy='constant', fill_value=0)
df_imputed = pd.DataFrame(imputer.fit_transform(df), columns=df.columns)
```

Becoming proficient in data analysis provides you with a number of different career opportunities and using Python as your go-to tool for data analysis streamlines this process. Making use of Python's extensive libraries like Pandas and NumPy allows for simplicity, readability, and user-friendliness. The significance of preprocessing and refining raw data for analysis shouldn't be overlooked, nor should the steps involved in this analysis.

In the chapters that follow, you'll learn the remainder of your critical Python lessons, steering you toward Python greatness and a world of career opportunities. While your active programming journey may be finished, I encourage you to continue to experiment, making use of our free gifts to further enhance your journey.

CHAPTER 10

Python Data Munging

Data munging is also known as data cleaning or data wrangling. This refers to the process of preparing your raw, unstructured data into a clean, structured format that is suitable for analysis. It's a crucial step in the data preparation pipeline and involves the transformation and manipulation of your data to make it more accurate, consistent, and ready for modeling. Some of the key aspects of data munging include,

- Handling missing data which includes identifying and addressing missing values.

- Dealing with duplicates and removing these.

- Data transformation which includes converting data types, scaling numerical features, and creating new variables.

- Handling outliers by identifying and addressing missing values.

- Normalizing data to ensure that it adheres to a standard scale.

- Addressing inconsistencies in naming conventions, formats, and units.

- Encoding and converting categorical variables into a numerical format for machine learning models.

- Feature engineering to create new features based on existing ones to enhance model performance.

What is important to note about data munging is that it is an iterative and exploratory process that is quite closely related to exploratory data analysis (EDA). When data munging is well-executed, it provides reliable and meaningful insights and ensures that the data reflects the true patterns and trends of the domain it represents.

Why Data Munging Is Important

Data munging is really important when it comes to data analysis and machine learning workflows. It addresses issues like missing values, duplicates, and outliers, and contributes to the overall quality and reliability of a specific dataset. Because clean data is absolutely fundamental to proper analysis and modeling, transforming and normalizing data ensures consistent and standardized outputs for meaningful and accurate results. When it comes to machine learning models, data munging enables the creation of relevant features and improves model interpretability, contributing to better model performance.

Because many machine learning models and algorithms have stringing requirements regarding data formats, data munging ensures that the data is prepared in a compatible manner with the chosen modeling techniques.

Addressing inconsistencies and biases in data during the munging process reduces the likeliness of bias errors in downstream analyses which is crucial for informed decision-making based on the data being presented. Clean and well-organized data is absolutely essential in the EDA process. This allows for analysts and scientists to explore relationships, patterns, and trends within a dataset, and allows for deeper data insights.

In real-world scenarios, data comes from a whole lot of different sources. In order for data to align with all of these different datasets, data munging allows for seamless integration for more comprehensive analysis.

In other words, data munging is the foundation for meaningful insights and building reliable data models. It transforms raw data into valuable assets, unlocking its true potential not only for decision-making purposes but for predictive modeling too.

Importing Datasets With Pandas

A fundamental step in the data analysis process is importing datasets with Pandas. This powerful library in Python is used for data manipulation and analysis, offering data structures like DataFrames that make it easier to handle structured data.

In this section, we're going to explore how to import datasets using Pandas.

Reading CSV Files

```
import pandas as pd

# Reading a CSV file into a DataFrame
df = pd.read_csv('your_dataset.csv')

# Displaying the first few rows of the DataFrame
print(df.head())
```

Reading Excel Files

```
# Reading an Excel file into a DataFrame
df_excel = pd.read_excel('your_dataset.xlsx', sheet_name='Sheet1')

# Displaying the first few rows of the DataFrame
print(df_excel.head())
```

Reading JSON Files

```
# Reading a JSON file into a DataFrame
df_json = pd.read_json('your_dataset.json')

# Displaying the first few rows of the DataFrame
print(df_json.head())
```

Reading SQL Tables

```
from sqlalchemy import create_engine

# Creating a SQLite database engine
engine = create_engine('sqlite:///your_database.db')

# Reading a SQL table into a DataFrame
df_sql = pd.read_sql('your_table', con=engine)

# Displaying the first few rows of the DataFrame
print(df_sql.head())
```

These codes above show you how to read datasets in various formats into Pandas DataFrames. Understanding these techniques is absolutely essential for any data analyst or junior scientist working with Python.

How to Preprocess Data With Pandas

Preprocessing data using Pandas is crucial to ensure that your data is clean and in a usable format for analysis and machine learning. Below are some of the most common data processing techniques using Pandas. Feel free to experiment with these codes yourself, munging your data appropriately.

Handling Missing Data

```
# Removing rows with missing values
df.dropna(inplace=True)

# Filling missing values with a specific value
df.fillna(value, inplace=True)
```

Removing Duplicates

```python
# Removing duplicate rows based on all columns
df.drop_duplicates(inplace=True)

# Removing duplicates based on specific columns
df.drop_duplicates(subset=['column1', 'column2'], inplace=True)
```

Transforming Data

```python
# Changing data types of columns
df['column_name'] = df['column_name'].astype('new_dtype')

# Applying a function to a column
df['column_name'] = df['column_name'].apply(your_function)
```

Handling Outliers

```python
lower_bound = df['column_name'].quantile(0.25) - 1.5 * df['column_name'].std()

upper_bound = df['column_name'].quantile(0.75) + 1.5 * df['column_name'].std()

df_filtered = df[(df['column_name'] > lower_bound) & (df['column_name'] < upper_bound)]
```

Encoding Categorical Outliers

```python
df_encoded = pd.get_dummies(df, columns=['categorical_column'])
```

Feature Scaling

```
from sklearn.preprocessing import StandardScaler

# Scaling numerical features
scaler = StandardScaler()
df[['numeric_column1', 'numeric_column2']] =
scaler.fit_transform(df[['numeric_column1', 'numeric_column2']])
```

Handling DateTime Data

```
# Converting a column to DateTime format
df['date_column'] = pd.to_datetime(df['date_column'])

# Extracting features from DateTime
df['year'] = df['date_column'].dt.year
df['month'] = df['date_column'].dt.month
```

Handling Text Data

```
df['text_column'] = df['text_column'].str.lower()
```

Your goal when it comes to analysis will affect the code and the characteristics of the data munging you're performing. You may need to apply a combination of techniques to ensure your data is modeling and exploration ready.

Data Selection With Pandas

When it comes to data selection with Pandas, your objective is to retrieve specific subset of data from a DataFrame based on a set of different conditions. While there are a number of different techniques you can use for data selection in Pandas, we've supplied the most common of these techniques below.

Selecting Columns

```
# Selecting a single column
column_data = df['column_name']

# Selecting multiple columns
selected_columns = df[['column1', 'column2']]
```

Selecting Rows

```
# Selecting rows based on a condition
filtered_data = df[df['column_name'] > threshold]

# Selecting rows using multiple conditions
filtered_data = df[(df['column1'] > threshold1) & (df['column2'] < threshold2)]
```

Selecting Specific Columns and Rows

```
# Using loc for label-based indexing
selected_data = df.loc[df['column_name'] > threshold, ['column1', 'column2']]

# Using iloc for integer-based indexing
selected_data = df.iloc[indices, [0, 1]]
```

Using Queries

```
selected_data = df.query('column_name > threshold')
```

Using isin()

```
selected_data = df[df['column_name'].isin(['value1', 'value2'])]
```

Using between()

```
selected_data = df[df['column_name'].between(lower_bound, upper_bound)]
```

Setting Conditions for Data Modification

```
df.loc[df['column_name'] > threshold, 'column_name'] = new_value
```

Data munging is an essential skill for data analysis and machine learning. Its significance shouldn't be overlooked, especially when it comes to wrangling raw data and structuring it into a reliable format, addressing missing values and duplicates, and dealing with inconsistencies.

With Pandas as your tool of choice, you have the opportunity to import diverse datasets that execute critical preprocessing techniques. Whether you're looking to handle missing data or encode categorical variables, the skills you've experimented with in this chapter will help you to shape data into its most potent and valuable form. While I completely understand that not everyone has a future in computer science planned, I do encourage you to explore the value and power of data munging.

CHAPTER 11

Python Data Munging/Wrangling Exercise

As I mentioned above, this hands-on exercise is not for everyone and while I do encourage experimentation and exploration, you're welcome to skip this exercise if data munging is not your metaphorical cup of tea.

For those of you who wish to stick around and give data munging a go, this exercise will provide you with a practical exercise to help put your understanding of data munging techniques to the test.

You will need to ensure that you are using Python and Pandas to uncover missing challenges, like missing values, duplicates, and inconsistent formats when completing this exercise.

Scenario

You have been provided with a dataset that contains information about customer transactions. This dataset, however, appears to have missing values. Your task for this exercise is to handle the missing data appropriately, ensuring the dataset is ready for further analysis.

Dataset

```
import pandas as pd

data = {
    'CustomerID': [1, 2, 3, 4, 5],
    'Product': ['A', 'B', None, 'A', 'C'],
    'Quantity': [3, None, 1, 2, 5],
    'Price': [10.0, 15.0, 20.0, None, 25.0]
}

df = pd.DataFrame(data)
```

Your Task

1. Take the time to identify and count the missing values in this dataset.

2. Make a decision on an appropriate strategy that can be used to handle the missing values in each of the columns.

3. Once you have decided on your strategy, implement it so that you can handle the missing values for each column.

4. Update the dataset.

Take your time and work through this exercise and remember that frustration can be cured with curiosity and working back on the information that you've learned in this chapter. Once you are ready, take a look at my solution below.

```
# Task 1: Identify and count missing values
missing_values = df.isnull().sum()

# Task 2: Decide on a strategy
# For 'Product', replace missing values with 'Unknown'
df['Product'].fillna('Unknown', inplace=True)
# For 'Quantity'
df['Quantity'].fillna(df['Quantity'].mean(), inplace=True)
# 'Price', fill missing values with the mean of the column
df['Price'].fillna(df['Price'].mean(), inplace=True)

# Task 3: Updated dataset
updated_df = df
```

How did you do in this exercise?

CHAPTER 12

Inheritance in Python to Clean Your Code

When it comes to object-oriented programming (OOP), inheritance is a fundamental concept. It allows a new class (subclass) or derived class to inherit attributes and methods from an existing class (parent or base class). This relationship facilitates code reuse as well as abstraction and the creation of hierarchical classes.

Before we continue with inheritance, we need to understand some basic terminology.

1. A base class or parent class is the existing class whose attributes and methods are to be inherited.

2. A derived class or subclass is the new class that will inherit the attributes and methods from a parent class.

3. A superclass is just another term for a base class.

4. A child class is another term used for a derived class.

There are a couple of reasons that inheritance is great. It allows for code reusability and leveraging the functionality of the base class. Derived classes can provide a specific implementation for a method that has already been defined in an existing base class. This allows for customization. Finally, inheritance supports the creation of abstract classes that have common features that can be shared among multiple subclasses.

Let's take a look at the syntax and an example.

```
# Base class attributes and methods
class BaseClass:

 # Derived class attributes and methods
class DerivedClass(BaseClass):
```

Example

```
class Animal:
    def speak(self):
        print("Animal speaks")

class Dog(Animal):
    def bark(self):
        print("Dog barks")

my_dog = Dog()

my_dog.speak()  # Output: Animal speaks
my_dog.bark()   # Output: Dog barks
```

In the example above, *Dog* is a derived class that inherits from the *Animal* base class. The *speak* method is inherited from the base class and the derived class introduces its own method, *bark*. This example clearly shows how inheritance fosters a modular and hierarchical approach to building software, enhancing both code organization and maintainability.

How to Implement Inheritance in Code

In experimenting with the example above, you'll have picked up a couple of key points when it comes to inheritance—it needs to be implemented by specifying the base class in the definition of the derived class. In this section we're going to look at another example, to solidify not only the syntax but also how to input this syntax.

For this example, we'll use *Vehicle* as the base class with a method *start_engine*.

Car will be the derived class that inherits from *Vehicle* and we will introduce its own method *honk*. The constructor of the bass class is called in the constructor of the derived class. We'll be using *super{}* for this constructor. Our objective is to demonstrate how the derived class inherits attributes and methods from the base class while also having its own specialized behavior. Let's get to it.

```python
class Vehicle:
    def __init__(self, brand, model):
        self.brand = brand
        self.model = model

    def start_engine(self):
        print(f"The {self.brand} {self.model}'s engine is now running.")

class Car(Vehicle):
    def __init__(self, brand, model, num_doors):
            super().__init__(brand, model)
        self.num_doors = num_doors

    def honk(self):
        print(f"The {self.brand} {self.model} with {self.num_doors} doors honks.")

my_vehicle = Vehicle("Generic", "Vehicle")
my_car = Car("Toyota", "Camry", 4)


my_vehicle.start_engine()
my_car.start_engine()

my_car.honk()
```

The Super Method

The super method is executed using *super()* and it is used to call a method from the parent class within a method of the child class. This allows the child class to invoke the method defined in the parent class. This is particularly useful when overriding methods.

This can be a difficult concept to wrap your head around so let's look at an example. In the example below, the *Car* class inherits from the *Vehicle* class and overrides the *start_engine* method. Inside the overridden method, *super().start_enging()* is used to call the *start_engine* methods of the parent class. This allows the child class to extend or customize the behavior of the parent class method without completely replacing the behavior.

Syntax

```
class ChildClass(ParentClass):
    def some_method(self):
        super().parent_method()
```

Example

```
class Vehicle:
    def start_engine(self):
        print("Engine started")

class Car(Vehicle):
    def start_engine(self):
        print("Car engine started")
        super().start_engine()

# Creating an instance of the derived class
my_car = Car()

# Calling the overridden method in the derived class
my_car.start_engine()
```

Using *super()* is extremely common in constructor methods. If you remember correctly, constructor methods are used with the syntax *(__init__)*. This ensures that the initialization code in the parent class is executed before the child class initialization code. This helps to maintain a clear and consistent inheritance hierarchy.

Inheritance in Action Exercise

We've come to the end of this chapter but we need to solidify the knowledge you have learned. In this exercise you're going to build a zoo simulation, creating classes to represent different animals using inheritance.

The following steps are required.

1. Create a base class Animal with attributes name and species.

2. Include a method make_sound that prints a generic animal sound.

3. Create a derived class Mammal that inherits from Animal.

4. Add a method give_birth to represent the birthing process.

5. Create another derived class Bird that inherits from Animal.

6. Add a method *fly* to simulate a bird's ability to fly.

Once you have imputed your code, feel free to check back for the solution and my own code. Alternatively, if you are battling, have a look at and use the code below.

```python
# Base Class
class Animal:
    def __init__(self, name, species):
        self.name = name
        self.species = species

    def make_sound(self):
        print(f"{self.name} makes a generic animal sound.")

# Derived Class 1
class Mammal(Animal):
    def give_birth(self):
        print(f"{self.name} the {self.species} gives birth to live young.")

# Derived Class 2
class Bird(Animal):
    def fly(self):
        print(f"{self.name} the {self.species} takes flight.")

# Creating instances and testing
lion = Mammal("Leo", "Lion")
sparrow = Bird("Sunny", "Sparrow")

# Output: Leo makes a generic animal sound.
lion.make_sound()
# Output: Leo the Lion gives birth to live young.
lion.give_birth()

# Output: Sunny makes a generic animal sound.
sparrow.make_sound()
# Output: Sunny the Sparrow takes flight.
sparrow.fly()
```

And now you have the ability to use inheritance in your coding. As with your other exercises, it's a good idea to continue to practice, expanding upon your code and improving your skills. Make sure that you are saving your work often and coding in chunks that make it easy for you to pick up mistakes that may have been made and finetune your work.

CHAPTER 13

Integrating AI and Python Program

There is no doubt that artificial intelligence (AI) has revolutionized not only the world we live in but also the way we approach problems and decisions when it comes to programming and computer science. Python, with its simplicity, versatility, and a huge variety of powerful libraries and tools that are specifically designed for machine learning makes it the obvious choice for AI development.

When Python and AI are combined, it enhances the accessibility and efficiency of these two sciences, allowing for an innovative approach to AI programming. There are a number of benefits to using Python and these include

- a rich ecosystem of frameworks and libraries that we'll cover later in this chapter. These are specifically designed for AI and machine learning, simplifying complex AI implementations and allowing you to focus on logic.

- Python has a large, supportive community who values collaboration. This allows you access to knowledge and a means to solve problems quickly and efficiently.

- Python's easy-to-understand readable syntax makes it an ideal choice for the complexities of AI development. The simplicity of Python's language means developers can express AI concepts with ease and understanding. What this means is that beginners can also dip their toes into AI waters without having to learn complex ideas.

- when it comes to data science, Python has become the go-to language. Because AI relies so heavily on data, the seamless integration that Python offers when it comes to science tools and libraries allows for a smooth transition between AI implementation and data processing and analysis.

- AI requires scalability and Python is built on scalability. This ensures the language works well with AI applications, handling large datasets with ease and permitting evolution without ever sacrificing the performance of a project.

The simplicity of Python, as well as the power and cutting-edge libraries and tools, allow developers to unlock a world of possibilities that are driven by innovation. With the contribution of a vibrant community, new developers are able to access the world of AI programming with ease and simplicity.

Python AI Libraries

Python provides users with a huge variety of libraries and tools and when it comes to AI, Python certainly doesn't disappoint. As a language, Python has become the number one choice for AI development, allowing for a number of different facets when it comes to machine and deep learning and data science. It's important to note that Python provides users with an extraordinarily large number of tools and libraries and while we'd love to cover them all, we'd need to write an entirely new book. In this chapter, we'll explore the top four most popular of these libraries, uncovering each of their powerful capabilities.

TensorFlow

This open-source library was developed by Google for numerical computation and machine learning. It excels in building and training deep neural networks and boasts features like graphic-based computation and efficient modeling, support for both CPU and GPU acceleration, and a comprehensive ecosystem for machine learning tasks.

To access TensorFlow, install using the following command in your terminal.

- pip install tensorflow

This will install the latest stable version of TensorFlow but, if you need a specific version, you can specify it in your command.

You'll need to verify your installation once you have installed it. This can be done by inputting the following command.

- import tensorflow as tf

- print("TensorFlow version:", tf.__version__)

This will import TensorFlow and print its version.

Now that you have installed TensorFlow, you can start using it in Python. We'll provide you with an example of creating a TensorFlow constant and running session below.

```
import tensorflow as tf

hello = tf.constant("Hello, TensorFlow!")

with tf.compat.v1.Session() as session:

    result = session.run(hello)
    print(result.decode())
```

This will create a TensorFlow constant and run the session to evaluate and then print the constant's value. Always remember that as TensorFlow evolves there will be changes made and newer versions will be made available to users. Best practice when it comes to using Python Libraries is to refer to the official TensorFlow documentation and information.

Keras

API began as a separate high-level neural network that quickly became an integral part of TensorFlow. It provides users with an easy-to-use interface for building and training neural networks. Key features include simplified syntax for rapid prototyping, modular design for easy extension and customization, and integration with various backends, including TensorFlow.

If you have downloaded TensorFlow, you already have access to Keras. A reminder of how to install Tensorflow.

- pip install tensorflow

You can import the Keras module from TensorFlow with the following command,

- from tensorflow import keras

Now you can build a high-level API for building and training neural networks. Below is a simple example of how you can create a basic neural network using Keras.

```
from tensorflow import keras

from tensorflow.keras import layers

model = keras.Sequential([
    layers.Dense(128, activation='relu', input_shape=(784,)),
    layers.Dropout(0.2),
    layers.Dense(10, activation='softmax')
])

model.compile(optimizer='adam', loss='sparse_categorical_crossentropy', metrics=['accuracy'])
```

This example demonstrates a sequential model that is defined with one hidden layer, a dropout layer, and an output layer. The model is then compiled with an optimizer, loss function, and metrics.

Next, you'll need to train and evaluate your model. This can be done by using your dataset and evaluating its performance.

```
model.fit(x_train, y_train, epochs=5, validation_data=(x_val, y_val))

test_loss, test_acc = model.evaluate(x_test, y_test)
print("Test accuracy:", test_acc)
```

You'll need to replace the *x_train, y_train, x_value, y_value, x_test,* and *y_test* with your actual training, validation, and test datasets if you're going to use this example.

While this is a basic example of Keras, it demonstrates how much flexibility and customization is possible. As with TensorFlow, always refer to the official Keras documentation for more detailed features, and keep in mind that as the API evolves, new documentation will become available to you.

PyTorch

PyTorch was originally developed by Facebook. It's a dynamic deep learning framework that is known for its flexibility and user-friendliness. The research and development industry is particularly fond of PyTorch because of its dynamic computational graph for more intuitive model building, strong support for dynamic and static neural networks, active community and excellent documentation.

You can install PyTorch by using the following command,

- pip install torch

After installation, you'll need to verify that PyTorch is installed.

- import torch
- print("PyTorch version:", torch.__version__)

Once you have downloaded and verified PyTorch you can start using your Python scripts. Below is an example of creating a PyTorch tensor.

```
import torch
x = torch.tensor([[1, 2, 3], [4, 5, 6]])
print(x)
```

You can now begin to build and train your neural network. I'll give you another example.

```python
import torch
import torch.nn as nn
import torch.optim as optim

class SimpleNet(nn.Module):
    def __init__(self):
        super(SimpleNet, self).__init__()
        self.fc = nn.Linear(784, 10)

    def forward(self, x):
        x = self.fc(x)
        return x

model = SimpleNet()

criterion = nn.CrossEntropyLoss()
optimizer = optim.SGD(model.parameters(), lr=0.01)
```

You'll now need to train and evaluate your model.

```python
# Train the model with training data
for epoch in range(5):
    for inputs, labels in train_loader:
        outputs = model(inputs)
        loss = criterion(outputs, labels)

        optimizer.zero_grad()
        loss.backward()
        optimizer.step()

# Evaluate the model with test data
correct = 0
total = 0

with torch.no_grad():
    for inputs, labels in test_loader:
        outputs = model(inputs)
        _, predicted = torch.max(outputs.data, 1)
        total += labels.size(0)
        correct += (predicted == labels).sum().item()

print("Accuracy: {:.2f}%".format(100 * correct / total))
```

In this example you'll need to replace *train_loader* and *test_loader* with your actual data loaders to test your code.

Scikit-Learn

This versatile machine learning library provides simple yet efficient tools for data modeling and analysis. It is built on NumPy, SciPy, and Matplotlib. Key features of Scikit-Learn include, a consistent interface for various machine learning algorithms, extensive documentation and tutorials, and integration with other scientific computing libraries.

Accessing and using Scikit-Learn is pretty straightforward. The following command can be used to install Scikit-Learn.

- pip install scikit-learn

Once installed, you can import Scikit-Learn modules for specific tasks.

- from sklearn import datasets

- from sklearn.model_selection import train_test_split

- from sklearn.preprocessing import StandardScaler

- from sklearn.linear_model import LogisticRegression

- from sklearn.metrics import accuracy_score

Because Scikit-Learn provides tools for a number of different tasks, you'll need to apply whatever tool to your task—data preprocessing, feature extraction, model selection, and evaluation.

```python
# Load a dataset (for example, the iris dataset)
iris = datasets.load_iris()
X = iris.data
y = iris.target
# Split the dataset into training and testing sets
X_train, X_test, y_train, y_test = train_test_split(X, y, test_size=0.2, random_state=42)
# Standardize features by removing the mean and scaling to unit variance
scaler = StandardScaler()
X_train = scaler.fit_transform(X_train)
X_test = scaler.transform(X_test)
# Train a logistic regression classifier
model = LogisticRegression()
model.fit(X_train, y_train)
# Make predictions on the test set
y_pred = model.predict(X_test)
# Evaluate the model
accuracy = accuracy_score(y_test, y_pred)
print("Accuracy:", accuracy)
```

You'll need to replace the dataset and model with whatever it is your use is.

Scikit-Learn has extensive documentation that comes with detailed explanations as well as examples and tutorials. Make sure to refer to the official Scikit-Learn documentation when improving on your skills.

Collectively, these libraries empower AI developers to implement a number of solutions ranging from traditional machine learning to advanced deep learning models. Each of these libraries has its own strengths and weaknesses and it's up to you to experiment and find what works for you personally.

Defining Intelligence—The Five Prerequisites

Understanding the fundamental prerequisites of what makes AI what it is, is crucial for developing systems that can emulate a human-like intelligence. There are currently five prerequisites that define an intelligent system: reasoning, learning, problem-solving, and perception.

Reasoning involves the ability of a machine to analyze information and draw logical conclusions as well as make informed decisions. When it comes to AI, reasoning is implemented through algorithms that are designed to mimic human deductive and inductive reasoning. AI uses reasoning to assess situations, make decisions based on available data, and infer relationships.

Learning refers to AI's ability to improve its performance over a period of time by adapting new information it receives. Machine learning, while strictly a subset of AI, focuses on creating the algorithms that enable systems to learn patterns in behavior and make predictions based on these patterns. Learning algorithms are employed by a whole lot of AI applications including speech recognition, recommendation systems, and image classification.

Problem-solving is AI's capacity to analyze complex problems and devise effective solutions. AI leverages algorithms to simulate problem-solving abilities and can sometimes outperform humans in certain areas. AI-driven problem-solving is applied in optimization, planning, and logistics.

Perception is the ability to interpret information and make sense of it. AI uses computer vision, sensor data processing, and speech recognition to create perception. AI uses perception to recognize and understand spoken language, and objects, and in interpreting environmental data.

Finally, linguistic intelligence is the understanding and use of language effectively. In AI, natural language processing (NLP) techniques are used to both comprehend and generate human language. This is used in chatbots, language translation, and sentiment analysis.

These prerequisites are non-negotiable. AI aims to replicate the functionalities of the human brain and while not there yet, also human cognition. AI developers can therefore craft systems that not only display these five prerequisites but also diversify the areas which AI can be used in.

Agents and Environments in AI

When it comes to AI, understanding the dynamics between agents and environments. An agent is an entity that perceives an environment and takes action as well as receives feedback. An environment, on the other hand, encompasses the external context in which an agent operates. This interaction forms the foundation of any intelligent system. Now, I know this sounds confusing, so let's examine each of these aspects individually.

Agents are defined as autonomous entities that are capable of perceiving an environment. Agents do this to make decisions and take actions so that certain objectives are achieved. Attributes of agents include

- perception: Agents receive information about their environment through sensors.
- decision-making: Agents process the perceived information to make decisions.
- action: Agents execute actions based on their decisions.
- objective: Agents have specific goals or objectives to accomplish.

Environments, on the other hand, represent the external context in which an agent operates. This means an environment includes everything outside of an agent that could possibly be influenced or can influence an agent's actions. Types of environments include

- fully observable: The agent has access to the complete state of the environment.
- partially observable: The agent has limited information about the environment.
- deterministic: The next state is entirely determined by the current state and the agent's actions.

- stochastic: There is uncertainty in the outcome of actions due to randomness or external factors.

Interaction between agents and environments can occur as

- perception-action cycles: Agents continuously perceive the environment, make decisions based on the perceived information, take actions, and receive feedback from the environment.

- feedback: The environment provides feedback in the form of rewards, penalties, or changes in state, influencing the agent's future decisions.

Understanding how the agent-environment interaction occurs is fundamental if you want to design intelligent systems, especially in reinforcement learning scenarios. In reinforcement learning, agents learn optimal behaviors by receiving feedback in the form of rewards and punishments.

Clustering and Association

Clustering and association are crucial concepts when it comes to effective data analysis and decision-making in AI. Clustering and association offer valuable insights into the underlying structure and relationships with your data.

Clustering is the grouping of similar data points together based on certain features and characteristics. The goal of clustering is to identify inherent structures or patterns within the data. Its uses include

- customer segmentation based on purchasing behavior.

- image segmentation for object recognition.

- document clustering for topic modeling.

Techniques include

- K-means clustering—divides data into 'k' clusters based on mean values.

- Hierarchical clustering—forms a hierarchy of clusters.

Association is a form of analysis that aims to discover relationships, dependencies, or patterns that occur among variables in large datasets. Association identifies rules that describe the association between variables. Its uses include

- market basket analysis to understand customer buying patterns.

- recommend systems to suggest products or content.

- fraud detection by identifying unusual patterns in transactions.

Techniques include

- Apriori algorithm—finds frequent itemsets to generate association rules.

- FP-growth algorithm—efficiently mines frequent patterns.

These two aspects differentiate in a couple of ways including nature, objectives, and output. Clustering deals with grouping similar data points while association focuses on identifying rules and relationships. Likewise, the objectives and outputs differ. Let's look at an example to help understand these two better.

Clustering groups customers with similar purchase behavior when it comes to customer data whereas association reveals the rules, like "Jane Doe buys shoes but also tends to buy socks at the same time." This allows AI to suggest products to Jane Doe not just based on her likes but also on what her associated buying trends are.

Machine Learning Algorithms

AI relies on machine learning (ML) as it is the foundation for computers to learn from data and improve performance over time and without explicit programming. Algorithms and computational procedures that discover patterns, optimize decisions, and make decisions are at the heart of machine learning.

Key concepts of machine learning include supervised, unsupervised, and reinforcement learning. Let's break these down.

Supervised Learning

In supervised learning training on labeled datasets occurs. Each input is associated with a corresponding output and the goal is to learn a mapping function that will accurately predict an output for unseen and new inputs.

Unsupervised Learning

The exploration of data without labeled outputs is referred to as unsupervised learning. Algorithms aim to discover hidden patterns as well as group data points and reduce the dimensionality of a data set.

Reinforcement Learning

Reinforcement learning models learn by interacting with their environment. These models receive feedback in the form of rewards and punishment (penalties), and this allows them to adapt and optimize their behavior over time.

The algorithms used in machine learning differ as well and include

- classification algorithms—assign inputs to predefined categories, for example, spam detection.

- regression algorithms—predict continuous values, for example, programs that predict inflation.

- clustering algorithms—group similar data points based on features.

- dimensionality reduction algorithms—simplify datasets while retaining essential information.

Algorithms play an instrumental role in applications including natural language processing, image recognition, autonomous vehicles, and so on. When we understand the huge variety of roles these algorithms play, we can grasp just how important they are in AI and machine learning. It also highlights the importance of knowing what the most commonly used of these algorithms are as well as their strengths and weaknesses.

Logistic Regression

Logistic Regression is a supervised machine learning algorithm used for binary and multi-class classification. Despite its name, it is primarily employed for classification tasks rather than regression.

Key Concepts

Binary classification—logistic regression predicts the probability that an instance belongs to a particular class. The outcome is then transformed into a binary decision, usually using a threshold.

Sigmoid Function

The logistic function (sigmoid function) is crucial for logistic regression. It maps any real-valued number to the range of [0, 1], making it suitable for representing probabilities.

Sigmoid function is denoted by the theorem

$$\sigma(z) = \frac{1}{1+e^{-z}}$$

The decision boundary separates different classes in the input feature space. It is a hyperplane determined by the model parameters. Logistic regression uses the cross-entropy loss function to measure the difference between predicted probabilities and actual class labels.

Training Process

Initialization—initialize weights and biases.

Forward propagation—compute the weighted sum of inputs and apply the sigmoid function to get predicted probabilities.

Loss computation—calculate the cross-entropy loss between predicted and actual probabilities.

Backpropagation—update weights and biases using gradient descent to minimize the loss.

Repeat—iterate through steps 2-4 until convergence.

Used In

- Spam detection
- Credit scoring
- Medical diagnosis
- Customer churn prediction
- Image categorization

Logistic regression is a foundational algorithm when it comes to classification, providing a clear understanding of how input features contribute to the predicted probabilities. It serves as a fundamental building block in many machine learning applications.

Decision Tree

Decision trees are widely used machine learning algorithms that can be applied to regression and classification tasks. To make decisions, decision trees work recursively, splitting datasets based on features to make decisions.

Key Concepts

- There are a number of key concepts when it comes to decision trees. These include
- Decision nodes—nodes in a decision tree represent decisions or test conditions based on input features. A decision node asks a question about a feature, leading to different branches.
- Leaf nodes—leaf nodes represent the final outcomes or class labels. Each path from

the root to a leaf represents a decision path.

- Information gain (entropy)—decision trees use metrics like entropy to determine the best feature for splitting the data. Information gain measures the reduction in uncertainty (entropy) after a dataset is split.

- Gini impurity—another criterion for splitting is Gini impurity, which measures the likelihood of misclassifying a randomly chosen element.

- Splitting criteria—decision Trees recursively split the dataset based on features to create homogeneous subsets.

Training Process

- Initialization—build the tree starting from the root node.

- Splitting—select the feature that provides the best split (highest information gain or lowest Gini impurity).

- Recursive process—repeat the process for each subset, creating branches until a stopping criterion is met (e.g., reaching a maximum depth).

- Leaf node assignment—assign a class label to each leaf node.

Used In

- Fraud Detection
- Customer Segmentation
- Medical Diagnosis
- Predictive Maintenance
- Image Classification

A Word on Random Forests

Random forests are groups of decision trees. They build multiple trees and combine their predictions to improve accuracy and reduce overfitting.

If you've ever created a mind map, you'll see the similarity between decision trees and this human cognitive decision-making technique. In AI decision trees provide a transparent, intuitive way for a machine to make decisions on input features. While single decision trees are often ineffective, techniques that include pruning and ensemble methods like random forests enhance the performance of the machine's learning capabilities.

Support Vector Machine

Support vector machines (SVM) are powerful supervised learning algorithms. These are used for classification and regression tasks and the aim of SVMs is to find the hyperplane that best separates data points into different classes. This maximized the margin between classes.

Key Concepts

- Hyperplane—SVM hyperplanes are decision boundaries that separate data points belonging to different classes. For two-dimensional data, the hyperplane is a line, and for three-dimensional data, it's a plane.

- Margin—the margin is the distance between the hyperplane and the nearest data points from each class.

- Support vectors—these are the data points that lie closest to the hyperplane and influence its position. These points are critical for defining the margin.

- Kernel trick—for the efficient handling of non-linear decision boundaries, kernel tricks are used to map input features into a higher-dimensional space. Common kernels include linear, polynomial, radial basis function (RBF), and sigmoid.

Training Process

Feature mapping—if it's needed, map input features are inputted into higher-dimensional space using a kernel function.

Optimization—the hyperplane is found to maximize the margin while minimizing classification errors.

Decision function—the trained model now predicts the class of new data points based on their position relative to the hyperplane.

Used In

- Image classification
- Handwriting recognition
- Text classification
- Bioinformatics
- Fraud detection

SVMs are extremely useful when having to deal with complex decision boundaries and datasets that have high dimensionality.

Naive Bayes

Okay, things are going to get a little more complicated for this last section. If you don't 100% understand what we're talking about, that's perfectly fine. The technical terms aren't as important as the actual coding. Once you begin to use machine learning, it'll be much easier to understand and implement what has been taught.

Naive Bayes is a family of probabilistic classification (theory of probability) algorithms based on Bayes' theorem. It assumes that features are conditionally independent, which simplifies the computation and leads to a *naive* assumption.

Key Concepts

Naive Bayes uses Bayes' theorem to calculate the probability of a hypothesis (class label) based on the observed evidence (features). This is denoted by the theorem,

$$P(A|B) = \frac{P(B|A) \cdot P(A)}{P(B)}$$

- Conditional independence—the naive assumption in Naive Bayes is that features are conditionally independent given the class label. Despite its simplifying assumption, Naive Bayes often performs well in practice.

Naive Bayes has three types. These include,

- Multinomial Naive Bayes—suitable for discrete data, often used in text classification (e.g., document categorization).

- Gaussian Naive Bayes—assumes features follow a normal distribution and is appropriate for continuous data.

- Bernoulli Naive Bayes—designed for binary features, commonly used in document classification.

Training Process

Data preparation—calculate class probabilities and conditional probabilities for each feature given to the class.

Prediction—for a new instance, calculate the posterior probability for each class and choose the class with the highest probability.

Used In

- Email spam detection

- Text classification
- Sentiment analysis
- Medical diagnosis
- Fraud detection

Naive Bayes is particularly popular for text classification tasks, such as spam filtering and sentiment analysis. Its simplicity and efficiency make it a go-to choice for coders.

K-Nearest Neighbors

K-Nearest Neighbors (KNN) is a versatile and simple machine learning algorithm used for both classification and regression tasks. It makes predictions based on the majority class or average of neighboring data points.

Key Concepts

- Distance metric—KNN relies on a distance metric to measure the similarity between data points. Common distance metrics include Euclidean, Manhattan, Minkowski, and Hamming.

- K-Neighbors—KNN considers the 'k' nearest neighbors to a data point to make predictions. The choice of 'k' impacts the model's sensitivity to noise and overall performance.

- Majority voting—for classification, the class that appears most frequently among the 'k' neighbors is assigned to the new data point.

- Mean (regression)—for regression, the average of the 'k' nearest neighbors' target values is assigned to the new data point.

Training Process

- Store training data—KNN stores the entire training dataset.

- Prediction—for a new data point, calculate distances to all training points and identify the 'k' nearest neighbors. Make predictions based on majority voting (classification) or mean (regression).

Used In

- Handwriting recognition
- Image classification
- Recommender systems
- Anomaly detection
- Predicting medical diagnoses

A Word on Choosing 'k'

- A smaller 'k' increases model sensitivity to noise but may be more accurate for intricate patterns.
- A larger 'k' provides a smoother decision boundary but may overlook local patterns.

K-Nearest Neighbors is a straightforward algorithm suitable for a whole lot of different scenarios. Its effectiveness lies in its simplicity and flexibility, making it a valuable tool for quick predictions in both classification and regression tasks.

K-Means Clustering

K-Means is an unsupervised machine learning algorithm. It is used for clustering similar data points into distinct groups or clusters. This is done by partitioning the dataset into 'k' clusters, where each data point belongs to the cluster with the nearest mean.

Key Concepts

- Centroids—K-Means identifies 'k' centroids, initially placed randomly or determined by a specific initialization method. A centroid represents the mean of data points within its cluster.

- Assigning data points—each data point is assigned to the cluster whose centroid is closest in terms of Euclidean distance.

- Updating centroids—after all data points are assigned, the centroids are recalculated as the mean of the data points within each cluster.

- Iterations—assigning points and updating centroids is repeated until convergence.

- Convergence—occurs when centroids no longer change significantly or after a predetermined number of iterations.

Training Process

- Initialization—randomly select 'k' data points as initial centroids or use a specific initialization method.

- Assign data points—assign each data point to the nearest centroid, forming 'k' clusters.

- Update centroids—calculate the centroids based on the mean of data points in each cluster.

- Repeat steps 2-3 until convergence.

Used In

- Customer segmentation

- Document classification

- Image compression

- Anomaly detection

- Genetics

A Word on Determining 'k'

The choice of 'k' is critical and may involve methods like the Elbow Method or Silhouette Analysis. Keep this in mind when using K-means clustering.

K-means clustering is widely used for data exploration and pattern recognition. It's fairly simple and extremely efficient, making it great for scenarios where the number of clusters is known or needs to be determined based on the data's inherent structure.

Building Your First Classifier in Python

We've reached the end of this chapter and your penultimate exercise. As with the other exercises in these final three chapters, the application is very specific to data science, AI, and machine learning. If this is something that doesn't interest you, please feel free to skim over the exercise. Having said that, I do suggest testing it out so that you can put your knowledge to the test.

In this exercise, you're going to build a simple classifier using one of the discussed algorithms (Naive Bayes, KNN, or SVM) to classify a dataset into two or more classes. For the solution below, we've used Naive Bayes.

Instructions

1. Choose a dataset—select a dataset suitable for classification. You can use popular datasets like the Iris dataset for simplicity.

2. Data exploration—load and explore the dataset to understand its features and structure.

3. Data preprocessing—if needed, preprocess the data by handling missing values, encoding categorical variables, or scaling features.

4. Choose a classifier—select one of the classification algorithms discussed (Naive Bayes, KNN, or SVM).

5. Train-test split—split the dataset into training and testing sets.

6. Train the classifier—train the selected classifier on the training set.

7. Evaluate the model—use the testing set to evaluate the performance of your model. Consider metrics like accuracy, precision, recall, and F1 score.

Give it a try and try to debug any issues you may come across. When you are ready, the solution, using Naive Bayes, is below.

Solution

```python
# Example using Naive Bayes (you can replace this with KNN or SVM)
from sklearn.model_selection import train_test_split
from sklearn.naive_bayes import GaussianNB
from sklearn.metrics import accuracy_score, classification_report

# Load and explore the dataset (replace 'X' and 'y' with your features and target variable)
from sklearn.datasets import load_iris
data = load_iris()
X, y = data.data, data.target

# Train-test split
X_train, X_test, y_train, y_test = train_test_split(X, y, test_size=0.2, random_state=42)

# Choose a classifier (Naive Bayes)
classifier = GaussianNB()

# Train the classifier
classifier.fit(X_train, y_train)

# Make predictions on the test set
y_pred = classifier.predict(X_test)

# Evaluate the model
accuracy = accuracy_score(y_test, y_pred)
report = classification_report(y_test, y_pred)

print(f"Accuracy: {accuracy}")
print("Classification Report:\n", report)
```

CHAPTER 14

Common Debugging Tools for Seamless Programming

Learning to debug is an absolutely critical skill. When you have the right tools, the process becomes more efficient and you don't spend an extraordinary amount of time trying to fix errors in your Python code.

Before we get into debugging tools though, we have something exciting for you.

A Free Gift For You

We know that bugs can be annoying! Python, while user-friendly can sometimes be perplexing, but we have you covered. This free gift has been designed as a quick reference guide when it comes to *Python Code Mistakes*. These top-most common bugs provide you with simple, effective solutions to your bugging issues. But that's not all! We've provided you with a space to write down your own solutions and common mistakes you make so that you always have a reference on hand.

Simply scan the QR code below to receive your copy of *Python Code Mistakes Uncovered*.

Python Debugging Tools

Unraveling the mysteries of a bug within your code can be infuriating. Picture this: you've crafted a masterpiece of logic and syntax only to run your program and a bug lights up your screen.

Debugging tools are designed to help you metaphorically squash those bugs, solving your confusion and offering a little bit of enlightenment. This section is going to take you through debugging, providing you with the tools to make your Python programming experience a little smoother and more enjoyable. Understanding these tools allows you to harness the full power of Python as a programming language, but first, let's examine why you need debugging tools in the first place.

Why Debugging Tools

Debugging tools are the magnifying glass used to ensure you can unravel the intricacies of your code. Python, while well-known for its readability and simplicity, can still have some pretty elusive bugs that can be difficult to wrap your mind around.

Debugging tools help you to create flawless code and provide you with a means to peer into the inner workings of your program so that you can identify issues and rectify them until your code is perfect. Along with your companion guide, *Python Code Mistakes Uncovered,* you can uncover everything from syntax errors to logical missteps as well as complex runtime issues. Now, before we dive into the specifics of each tool, we need to take a look at the debugging landscape as a whole, uncovering where some of these bugs occur and the stages at which debugging can occur.

1. Integrated Development Environments (IDEs)—IDEs like PyCharm, VSCode, and Jupyter Notebook provide an immersive coding experience with built-in debugging features.

2. Interactive Debuggers—Python offers interactive debuggers like PDB (Python Debugger) that allow you to step through your code, inspect variables, and gain insights in real-time. We'll uncover the power of these interactive debugging tools below.

3. Logging—logging is not just for recording events; it can be used as a strategic debugging tool that assists in tracing the flow of your program and identifying potential bottlenecks.

4. Profiling Tools—profiling tools like cProfile and Py-Spy help you analyze the performance of your code.

5. Error Tracking Services—sometimes your code can venture completely off-patch and error tracking services like Sentry and Rollbar become invaluable tools.

Each tool used in debugging has its own strengths and specialities. This means you can, and should, build your own personalized debugging toolkit. This will provide you with a set of instruments that align with not only your coding preferences but also with the nature of whatever project you're working on.

We've provided some of these tools below, but it's important that you understand that debugging is very much a case of, "Your toolbox, your rules."

Simple But Effective Debugging Tools

Print statements—simple yet effective, strategically placed print statements can help trace the flow of your program and inspect variable values at different stages.

Example

```python
def calculate_area(length, width):
    print(f"Calculating area for length: {length} and width: {width}")
    area = length * width
    print(f"Area calculated: {area}")
    return area

def main():
# Example usage
    rectangle_length = 5
    rectangle_width = 8

# Adding print statements for debugging
    print("Starting the main function")

# Call the calculate_area function
    result = calculate_area(rectangle_length, rectangle_width)

# Print the result
    print(f"Result: {result}")
    print("Exiting the main function")

if __name__ == "__main__":
    main()
```

Python Debugger (pdb)—Python comes with a built-in debugger called pdb. This debugger allows you to learn how to set breakpoints, step through code, and inspect variables interactively.

Example

```python
import pdb

def calculate_sum(a, b):
    result = a + b
    pdb.set_trace()  # Set breakpoint here
    return result

if __name__ == "__main__":
    x = 5
    y = 7
    total = calculate_sum(x, y)
    print(f"The total is: {total}")
```

Integrated Development Environments (IDEs)—IDEs like PyCharm, Visual Studio Code, and Jupyter Notebooks provide advanced debugging features, including breakpoints, variable inspection, and step-by-step execution.

Logging—utilize the logging module to record messages during program execution. Configurable logging can help diagnose issues without modifying the code.

Example

```
import logging

#Configuring the logging system
logging.basicConfig(level=logging.DEBUG, format='%(asctime)s - %(levelname)s - %(message)s')

#Logging messages
logging.debug('This is a debug message')
logging.info('This is an info message')
logging.warning('This is a warning message')
logging.error('This is an error message')
logging.critical('This is a critical message')

#Variable Data in Log Messages
user = 'Alice'
logging.info(f'User {user} logged in')

#Logging Exception Information
try:
    result = 10 / 0
except ZeroDivisionError:
    logging.error('Error occurred', exc_info=True)

#Logging to a File
file_handler = logging.FileHandler('my_log.log')
formatter = logging.Formatter('%(asctime)s - %(levelname)s - %(message)s')
file_handler.setFormatter(formatter)
logging.getLogger().addHandler(file_handler)

#Adjusting Logging Levels Dynamically
logging.getLogger().setLevel(logging.DEBUG)
```

Exception Handling—properly implement try-except blocks to catch and handle exceptions effectively. Logging or printing informative messages within except blocks helps in identifying issues with greater efficiency.

Example

```
try:

 # Code that might raise an exception
   result = 10 / 0
except Exception as e:

# Handle the exception
   print(f'An error occurred: {e}')
```

Assertions—use assert statements to enforce assumptions about your code. When an assertion fails, it indicates a potential issue that needs investigation.

Example

```
def divide(a, b):
    assert b != 0, "Cannot divide by zero"
    return a / b

# Example 1: Valid division
result1 = divide(10, 2)
print(result1)  # Output: 5.0

# Example 2: Division by zero (assertion fails)
result2 = divide(10, 0)
# Raises AssertionError with the message "Cannot divide by zero"
```

Debugging Best Practices

Debugging is the unsung hero when it comes to programming. No programmer is perfect, and I have personally had conversations with some of the industry greats who have said, "Narry, we spend 95% of our day debugging and Googling an issue. The rest of the 5% is coffee and coding!"

Bugs happen, it's just an inevitable part of the coding process and while you do have the tools to debug your coding, you'll also need to know debugging best practices. The universal truth when it comes to programming is that bugs are here to stay, but how we approach these bugs can make all the difference.

So the first thing I'd like you to know is that debugging is not just about fixing errors; it's about understanding what went wrong with your code. This allows you to identify patterns, and craft proper solutions. This also means that you need to tap into your strategic mindset. It's this way of thinking that will encourage you to approach bugs with a structured plan rather than failing frustratingly.

Tips for Effective Debugging

1. Isolate the problem—identify the specific part of the code causing issues. Narrow down the problem to make debugging more focused and time-efficient.

2. Read error messages—Python is a simple language which means it's easy to understand error messages and tracebacks. These often provide valuable information about the nature of the problem.

3. Step through code—use debugging tools to step through your code one line at a time. This allows you to examine variable values at each step to pinpoint errors.

4. Consult documentation—refer to documentation for libraries and modules you're using. This helps you to understand expected behaviors and can uncover misunderstandings.

- Collaborate—one of the greatest selling factors when it comes to Python is its huge, engaging, and friendly community. When in doubt, make sure to seek out help from these online communities. Another perspective can often help you identify problems you may have overlooked.

Final Exercise

We've reached your final exercise using Python. In this exercise, you're going to a simple contact management system using Python. Your program should have the following features:

Add a Contact

- Allow users to add a new contact with details such as name, phone number, and email.

View Contacts

- Display a list of all contacts with their details.

Search for a Contact

- Implement a search functionality that allows users to find a contact by entering a name.

Delete a Contact

- Allow users to delete a contact by providing the contact's name.

Save Contacts to a File

- Implement a feature to save the contacts to a file so that users can load them later.

Load Contacts from a File

Implement a feature to load previously saved contacts from a file.

You have all the knowledge and tools to create this program, so go ahead, and when you are ready, look at our solution below.

Solution

```python
import json

class ContactManager:
    def __init__(self):
        self.contacts = []

    def add_contact(self, name, phone, email):
        contact = {'name': name, 'phone': phone, 'email': email}
        self.contacts.append(contact)
        print(f'Contact {name} added successfully.')

    def view_contacts(self):
        for contact in self.contacts:
            print(contact)

    def search_contact(self, name):
        for contact in self.contacts:
            if contact['name'] == name:
                print(f'Contact found: {contact}')
                return
        print(f'Contact with name {name} not found.')

    def delete_contact(self, name):
        for contact in self.contacts:
            if contact['name'] == name:
                self.contacts.remove(contact)
                print(f'Contact {name} deleted successfully.')
                return
        print(f'Contact with name {name} not found.')

    def save_contacts(self, filename='contacts.json'):
        with open(filename, 'w') as file:
            json.dump(self.contacts, file)
        print(f'Contacts saved to {filename}.')

    def load_contacts(self, filename='contacts.json'):
        try:
            with open(filename, 'r') as file:
                self.contacts = json.load(file)
            print(f'Contacts loaded from {filename}.')
        except FileNotFoundError:
            print(f'File {filename} not found. No contacts loaded.')

# Example Usage:
contact_manager = ContactManager()
contact_manager.add_contact('John Doe', '123-456-7890', 'john@example.com')
```

Conclusion

Congratulations reader! You're well on your way to becoming a Python master. From the fundamentals of the programming language to the intricacies of AI and machine learning, you now have all the tools and knowledge you need to become a Python programmer.

Python is renowned for its simplicity and versatility and this means the door has opened for you to enter a career in coding that is in incredibly high demand. In the first few chapters, you learned and gained a deeper understanding of syntax, data types, and basic programming constructs. You would have picked up just how readable Python's straightforward syntax is and kickstarted your coding journey with an easy-to-follow exercise.

As you became more familiar with Python's code, you delved into the world of variables, loops, and conditional statements, laying a solid foundation for your more complex programs. Functions were presented and you were able to begin creating code that was modular and reusable. You learned how to define, call, and pass parameters to functions. This allows you to both enhance the structure of your code as well as the efficiency of your program. Just how important functions are was further highlighted as we showed you the principles of procedural programming.

You've learned control flow mechanisms, including loops and conditional statements, allowing you to manipulate the execution of your code, and through iteration and making decisions, you are equipped with the tools you need to create a dynamic and responsive program.

As we moved into Python's more advanced programming structures, you were introduced to object-oriented programming (OOP). This would have marked a pivotal moment in your coding journey as concepts like classes, objects, and inheritance empowered you to design scalable and organized code. Python's absolute brilliance in implementing OOP principles has now enabled you to craft sophisticated programs and grasp the essence of software architecture.

And, as you entered into the world of data science, Python allowed you to begin delving into more advanced features. List comprehensions streamlined the creation of lists, generators enhanced efficiency in handling large datasets, and decorators allowed you to modify or extend the behavior of functions. You were introduced to Python's enormous libraries and tools on offer so that you could orient yourself with tools like NumPy and Pandas for data manipulation, and TensorFlow for machine learning. The ability to leverage existing libraries and frameworks truly allows programmers to tap into the versatility of Python, regardless of what a person wants to do with their code.

Finally, the exercises provided to you in this book serve as the columns for your success. They are documented examples of how far you have come in your Python coding journey. You're now ready to apply what you have learned about Python to the real world. From creating contact management systems to exploring data preprocessing and machine learning, you can now seamlessly translate theoretical knowledge into practical solutions.

Before closing the final page of this book, I'd like to remind you that your Python success is not only based on your knowledge but on the vibrant, inclusive community within this coding language. I encourage you to join and participate in this community so that you can share your experiences, contribute to open-source projects, and engage in discussions.

When joining the Python community, you learn a fundamental lesson—that coding is a lifelong journey. Technology evolves rapidly and this means that mastering Python is not the end of your journey in programming. You'll need to embrace a mindset that enjoys continual learning, stay curious, and explore emerging trends and technologies. The skills you've acquired here serve as a solid foundation for future learning and innovation but what you can learn has no limits.

One Last Word

Before you close this book, I'd like to take this opportunity to ask for your honest review and feedback. Your opinion helps me to improve my future books and ensures my readers are getting what they need from their reading experience.

Simply scan the QR code below and supply me with your feedback; and thank you for joining me on this coding journey. May your Python adventures continue to unfold, leading you to new horizons and discoveries. Happy coding!

Printed in Great Britain
by Amazon